the RAMADAN COOKBOOK

the RAMADAN COOKBOOK

80 Delicious Recipes Perfect for Ramadan, Eid, and Celebrating throughout the Year

ANISA KAROLIA

Countryman Press

An Imprint of W. W. Norton & Company
Independent Publishers Since 1923

Contents

Introduction   6
What Ramadan Means to Me   9

Something for Suhoor   **11**
Satisfying Small Bites   **25**
Comforting Classics   **53**
Fusion Flavors   **75**
Perfect for a Feast   **97**
Salads, Breads & Chutneys   **121**
So Refreshing   **139**
Everything Sweet   **149**

My Desi Pantry   164
My Favorite Spice Mixes   168
Reader Recipes   170
Acknowledgments   184
Index   185

Introduction

Growing up in a family of foodies, cooking and talking about recipes has always been a major part of life for me. My earliest fondest memories are of spending my summer vacations and free time with my beloved late grandmother, Mariam. She was one of the earliest Indian settlers in Leicester, in England, in the 1950s; she was very kind and generous and would give everyone in the neighborhood invites (Dawat) to the house to eat. For that reason, she was very well known and loved and, to this day, is still remembered by so many people I meet.

I was fortunate and blessed to have spent lots of my spare time with my gran, especially in the kitchen. Her cooking combined influences from Indian culture (from where she moved to the United Kingdom), and the Malawi style of cooking (where she was born and grew up). I remember just before iftar in Ramadan, she would tell me to wait a few more minutes while she fried up fresh pakoras or samosas to give to the neighbors. Or she'd give some to me to take back home, which I did with a big grin as I took charge of a plate of hot deliciousness wrapped in paper towels. It's a tradition I carry on to this day, sending our kids to share food with our neighbors, so our kids also learn the values and importance of kindness and generosity. I'm sure many British Indian kids who grew up in the 1980s can relate to this! I guess that was the beginning of my beautiful relationship with food and cooking.

My dear mother, Amina, was born and bred in the United Kingdom, but had lots of experience perfecting the art of Indian cooking with my gran, who she'd help in the kitchen. I remember going through my mum's handwritten recipe books and making my own version of my favorite recipes. I would always be asking what she was cooking as soon as I stepped inside the house after school—the delicious aroma always made me smile as I walked through our home.

My early attempts at cooking, helping my mum in the kitchen, would often end up creating a mess—either in the kitchen or the dish itself! However, my mother never discouraged me and let me carry on learning from my mistakes. Folding a basic samosa triangle was so intimidating back then, and my roti were the irregular shapes of countries on a map. But before long and after lots of practice, they were nice and round! I tell these stories to so many youngsters: never be afraid of cooking, and keep trying. Help your parents in the

kitchen, follow a cookbook, watch a video—however you feel comfortable. You will surely create magic in the kitchen if you have the interest and appetite for it!

My father, Nazir, also has a great love of food and would often get involved, from finding the best-quality vegetables at the local grocery store (being fussy—he is good at that!) to giving his opinions on recipes and baking his speciality, Cardamom Cake, which he still makes to this day. It's really good, and it's delicious with a good cup of Indian chai!

I think one of the things that brought my husband, Adam, and I together was our shared love of good food. I already knew that my lovely mother-in-law, Yasmin, was an amazing and experienced cook, and her food was always well received and complimented by others. She spent her early years in Zomba, Malawi, and, like me, also spent time in the kitchen with her own dear mother. She was passionate about cooking from a young age and, like my own grandmother, she also loved cooking for guests, trying out new recipes, and often putting her own twist on things!

With this background, you can see how my influences and style of cooking have developed and evolved. Many of the dishes I make are from Surat, in India, but others are from Malawi or South Africa. I feel so fortunate to have been able to enjoy and learn how to cook amazing food, learning from so many experts and chefs in my own family.

After having my third child, I left my job with the intent to work from home. I absolutely loved art when I was at school, so I used my creative flair together with my passion for baking to start a cake business, posting a portfolio of my work on my Instagram. After a while, I started getting messages asking for baking advice or recipes for cakes—I really couldn't deny anyone good cake, so I started uploading my baking recipes.

It was at that point that I decided I wanted others to be able to enjoy great-tasting Indian food too, from my favorite meals from my own childhood to my family's regularly requested dishes today.

The previous generation was so experienced in cooking that they never really needed to write anything down, and I've heard so many people my age say that if they ever asked an elder for a recipe, the response was often, "Oh a bit of this and a bit of that." With this in mind, and at the suggestion of others, I started uploading full recipes on my Instagram account. This was at a time when food blogging wasn't even a thing. The recipes soon became very popular as I started with what seemed to me to be the most difficult dishes or the ones no one would share the recipe for, especially the Ramadan and Eid recipes! I wanted every person to be able to appreciate amazing food and to cook delicious, hearty dishes in the comfort of their own home without feeling intimidated by the whole process.

I slowly became known for sharing my authentic Indian dishes, those handed down through the generations, so everyone could enjoy the mouthwatering vibrant food I love. My friends and family soon suggested I start a YouTube channel and share video content for my recipes. Anyone who knows me will tell you how shy and conservative I am and I thought, *No way can I do that!* My earliest videos were very cheesy and cringeworthy, but with my husband Adam's help on the technical side of things (and his role as Chief Taster), we made it happen and have never looked back since.

For me, it was about trying to help and inspire people to create the incredible authentic recipes I grew up with. I think it's an important life skill for people to be able to make home-cooked food for themselves or their family. I love interacting with my audience, seeing their photos of the recipes they have re-created—the positive feedback actually inspires me to continue my journey of sharing creative and delicious recipes.

Among the recipes in this book are some that have stuck with me since childhood and others that are modern recipes with a twist. All can be enjoyed throughout Ramadan—from suhoor to iftar—including the celebration of Eid. The recipes are so versatile, though, that you and your family can enjoy the everyday meals in this book any time of year. I really do hope you enjoy these recipes as much as we do!

A note before we begin with the recipes. When oil is listed in the ingredients, you can use any flavorless oil (I use sunflower) unless otherwise specified.

What Ramadan Means to Me

· · · ✦ · · ·

Ramadan, for me, is about getting closer to my Creator.
It's about self-reflection, charity, sacrifice, family, and
thinking of those less fortunate. It's about fasting as a form
of physical and spiritual detox, giving me the opportunity to
engage with myself and really increase my God
Consciousness, removing bad habits and starting
some good ones.

Of course, food is also a big part of Ramadan, as Muslims
around the world abstain from eating between sunrise and
sunset, starting the day with the predawn meal of suhoor,
then spending time in the kitchen, usually with family
members, preparing something to eat for the evening.
There is also the tradition of distributing prepared food to
neighbors, sharing your blessings and sharing the love.

In Islam, cooking for your family is rewarded with blessings,
as you are sacrificing your time and energy to feed your
loved ones. With that in mind, to help you during
Ramadan, Eid, and in your everyday cooking throughout
the year, I have included in this book some of my favorite
tried-and-tested recipes with plenty of batch-cooking
ideas, so you can prepare meals in advance and freeze
them until required, freeing up some of your valuable time
for prayers and worship.

SOMETHING FOR

Suhoor

The word "suhoor" comes from the Arabic word *seher*, meaning the last third of the night. This is a social event in many Middle Eastern countries during Ramadan, with the whole family eating together. I've created some tasty, light, and energizing recipes to serve as a predawn meal. They are designed to nourish you, keep you going through the day, and set you up for the fasting ahead.

Caramelized Bananas on Brioche Toast

SERVES
1–2

TIME
**Prep: 5 minutes
Cook: 4 minutes**

Delicious, buttery, and sweet, this simple breakfast takes very little effort. Decadent caramelized bananas are served on crisp-on-the-outside and soft-on-the-inside brioche toast. This was my dad's favorite—we always had a bunch of bananas in the fruit basket. My dad made the best caramelized bananas, which he served warm with a drizzle of fresh cream and a slightly charred and crisp roti. A perfect breakfast, a tasty and filling way to start your day, and ready on the table in just 10 minutes.

Ingredients

CARAMELIZED BANANAS
2 tablespoons butter
2 tablespoons brown sugar
1 banana, halved lengthwise

BRIOCHE
¼ cup whole milk
1 egg, beaten
¼ teaspoon ground cinnamon
1 tablespoon brown sugar
1–2 slices brioche or white bread
1 tablespoon butter

Method

For the bananas, place a small frying pan over low heat, add the butter and sugar and heat for about 1 minute until the butter has melted and the sugar dissolved. Place the banana halves in the pan cut side down and cook for about 1 minute on each side until nice and golden brown, carefully using a spatula to turn the pieces, making sure not to smush them.

For the brioche, pour the milk into a bowl with the beaten egg, cinnamon, and sugar and whisk together. Dip the slice of brioche in the milk mixture and soak for 30 seconds on each side, just enough time to soak the egg mixture into the bread.

Melt the butter in another frying pan over low heat. Gently transfer the brioche to the pan, increase the heat slightly, and cook until golden brown, about 2 minutes on each side. Serve immediately, topped with the caramelized bananas and the sauce from the pan spooned on top.

 You could also add a dollop of whipped cream or clotted cream, a drizzle of maple syrup, or some fresh fruits and berries.

Date & Nut Slices

Start your day with these delicious, nutritious slices. Perfect for Ramadan, for suhoor or iftar, they are rich in vitamins and minerals and packed with lots of energy. These slices will help suppress sugar cravings and control your appetite throughout the day.

Ingredients

4 tablespoons (½ stick) butter
9 ounces pitted dates, finely chopped
¼ cup granulated sugar
1 ounce chopped pistachios
1 ounce chopped almonds
1 ounce chopped cashews
2 ounces Maria cookies or graham crackers, broken into pieces
sesame seeds, for sprinkling

Method

Melt the butter in a saucepan over low heat and add the dates and sugar. Cook until the dates soften and start to look mushy. This will take 8–10 minutes. Add the chopped nuts and cookies and stir everything together.

Take a sheet of parchment paper and lay it out flat. Sprinkle with sesame seeds and spread the date mixture on top. Roll into a log shape, using the paper to help make a tight roll. Chill in the fridge for 1 hour until firm, then cut into ½-inch slices. Store in an airtight container in the fridge for up to 2–3 weeks.

Banana, Date & Oat Smoothie

Naturally sweet, this smoothie is the perfect way to start your suhoor. So easy to whip up and made with just a handful of ingredients, it's rich in fiber, creamy, and satisfying.

Ingredients

1 banana
2 pitted Medjool dates
1 cup 2% milk
2 tablespoons rolled oats
½ teaspoon chia seeds

Method

Put all the ingredients in a blender and blend on high for 30–40 seconds until the ingredients are well combined and smooth. That's it! Pour and enjoy.

 You can use any milk you like—the recipe works just as well with whole milk or dairy alternative.

Folded Omelet with Cherry Tomatoes & Feta

SERVES
1

TIME
Prep: 5 minutes
Cook: 2 minutes

A simple yet satisfying omelet filled with juicy, sweet cherry tomatoes and tangy, crumbly feta. You can make this omelet any time of the day, but it makes a great breakfast, whatever you're doing. This will definitely keep you full for longer.

Ingredients

2 eggs
splash of milk
½ teaspoon salt
½ teaspoon pepper
½ teaspoon chili flakes
oil spray, for greasing
5–6 cherry tomatoes, quartered
2 ounces feta, crumbled

Method

Whisk the eggs in a bowl and add a splash of milk, the salt, pepper, and chili flakes.

Place a small frying pan over medium heat and spray in some oil to cover the base of the pan. Pour in the egg mixture and cook for 1 minute until the bottom sets. Sprinkle the tomatoes on one half of the omelet and crumble the feta on top. As the egg cooks, the edges will start to lift from the sides of the pan. Use a spatula to fold the other half of the omelet over the filling, cook for 1 minute more, and you're ready to serve.

 TIP You can try other fillings in this omelet, such as shredded Cheddar and spinach—or whatever appeals to you.

Shakshuka

SERVES 2

TIME
Prep: 10 minutes
Cook: 18 minutes

Shakshuka is a simple vegetarian dish, quick and easy to rustle up. The gently poached eggs nestle in a delicious chunky tomato and pepper sauce—it's so satisfying, you can serve it for breakfast, lunch, or even dinner. Serve with bread.

Ingredients

1 tablespoon olive oil
2 red onions, diced
½ red pepper, diced
1 fresh red chili, seeded and finely chopped
½ teaspoon mild chili powder
1 teaspoon sweet smoked paprika
1 teaspoon garlic paste
14 ounces chopped or plum tomatoes
4 eggs
salt
fresh cilantro leaves, chopped, to garnish

Method

Heat the oil in a frying pan over medium-low heat and add the onions. Cook for 3–5 minutes to soften, then add the red pepper, fresh chili, chili powder, paprika, and garlic paste. Stir in the tomatoes, season with salt, then bubble away for 8–10 minutes until nice and fragrant.

Using the back of a large spoon, make 4 dips in the sauce, then crack an egg into each one. Put a lid on the pan, then cook gently over low heat for 6–8 minutes until the eggs are done to your liking. Scatter with the cilantro leaves and serve.

 TIP You will need a frying pan with a lid for this dish. If you don't have a lid, cover the pan with foil instead.

Cheesy Chicken Muffins

MAKES
12

TIME
Prep: 20 minutes
Cook: 45 minutes

Soft, moist, cheesy, and super delicious, these savory muffins are great for a grab-and-go breakfast—so filling and so addictive.

Ingredients

2 tablespoons butter
11 ounces chicken breast, cut into ½-inch cubes
½ teaspoon dried mixed herbs
1 teaspoon garlic paste
½ teaspoon salt
1 teaspoon ground black pepper
2 cups all-purpose flour
1½ teaspoons baking powder
1 cup milk
2 ounces plain yogurt
1 large egg
7 ounces Cheddar, grated
2 tablespoons diced red pepper
2 tablespoons diced green pepper
2 tablespoons finely chopped spring onion
4 ounces canned corn, drained

Method

Preheat the oven to 350°F and line a 12-cup muffin tin with 5-inch squares of parchment paper.

Melt the butter in a saucepan over medium-low heat. Add the chicken, mixed herbs, garlic paste, salt, and pepper, cover, and cook for 15 minutes, or until the chicken is cooked through. Your kitchen will be smelling so good right now.

Whisk the flour with the baking powder in a large bowl. Whisk the milk with the yogurt and egg in a separate bowl, then pour the wet ingredients into the bowl with the dry ingredients. Add the cooked chicken, Cheddar, red and green peppers, spring onion, and corn and mix everything together until combined—the batter should be smooth and thick.

Divide the batter evenly among the cups in the muffin tin and cook in the oven for 30 minutes, or until the muffins are golden brown and crusty and spring back when touched. Cool in the tin for 10 minutes, then transfer to a cooling rack. Serve warm.

These muffins can be stored in the fridge for 4–5 days, so you can make them ahead of time. Warm them up in the microwave for 1 minute before serving.

 TIP Add a chopped red chili for a bit of kick if you like.

Fried Eggs with Peppers & Za'atar

SERVES

1–2

TIME

Prep: 5 minutes
Cook: 4 minutes

Fried eggs with a Middle Eastern twist, simple yet tasty. Za'atar is a very popular spice blend—herby, earthy, and fragrant. What I absolutely love about eggs is that they don't have to be boring; you can jazz them up with just about anything. Serve these delicious spicy fried eggs with toast to set you up for the day.

Ingredients

2 tablespoons unsalted butter
2 large eggs
1 tablespoon diced red pepper
1 tablespoon diced green pepper
1 tablespoon chopped spring onion
½ teaspoon salt
½ teaspoon ground black pepper
½ teaspoon chili flakes
½ teaspoon za'atar spice mix

Method

Melt the butter in a small frying pan over medium heat. Crack the eggs into the, pan and sprinkle the red and green peppers, spring onion, salt, black pepper, chili flakes, and za'atar on top. Cover and cook until the eggs are cooked to your liking—about 2 minutes for runny yolks or 4 minutes for well done. Serve immediately.

 TIP Pair up with sliced avocado and quartered cherry tomatoes, the perfect combo to start your day.

SATISFYING SMALL

Bites

These tasty little treats can be served before your main meal and, as the name suggests, they are totally satisfying and designed to take the edge off your hunger. These are my favorite bite-sized appetizers, ideal for serving to family or friends, or just as a treat for yourself. Most of them can be prepared in batches and frozen for a later date, ready to be cooked and eaten whenever you feel like a treat.

Spicy Potato & Corn Tortilla Samosas

SERVES
8–10

TIME
Prep: 45 minutes
Cook: 14 minutes

There is something so satisfying about a good old-fashioned vegetarian samosa. My samosas, with spicy potatoes and corn, are wrapped in ready-made tortillas, so you're good to go in no time at all! These can be enjoyed any time—they are perfect for batch-cooking and freezing, so ideal for iftar, but they are delicious throughout the year.

Ingredients

1 large potato, peeled and cut into ½-inch cubes
7 ounces canned corn, drained
1 teaspoon green chili paste
1 teaspoon garlic paste
1 teaspoon chili powder
1 teaspoon hot paprika
1 teaspoon ground cumin
½ teaspoon salt
½ teaspoon ground black pepper
½ teaspoon nigella seeds
4 ounces mozzarella, grated
2 tablespoons all-purpose flour
8 tablespoons water
4–5 tortillas, cut in half
oil, for deep-frying

Method

Boil the potatoes for 8–10 minutes until only just tender, then drain in a colander and set aside.

Place the corn in a bowl with the chili paste, garlic paste, chili powder, paprika, cumin, salt, black pepper, nigella seeds, and mozzarella. Add the potatoes and mix everything together, mushing the mixture with the back of a spoon a little, but not completely, to add some texture to the mixture.

Make a paste by mixing the flour and water in a small bowl to a smooth consistency.

Take one of the tortilla halves and use a pastry brush to brush a little of the flour paste around the edges. Place 2 tablespoons of the filling on one half of the tortilla and fold the other half over the top to form a triangle, as shown on page 31. Gently press around the edges of the samosa to make sure it's sealed properly, then repeat with the remaining tortillas and filling.

Heat the oil for deep-frying in a large saucepan over medium-high heat until it reaches 350°F. Fry the samosas in batches for 1 minute on each side until golden brown all over, then drain on paper towels. These are best eaten fresh on the day they are cooked.

 TIP These samosas can also be baked. Brush with a little oil and bake in a preheated oven at 350°F for 10–15 minutes.

Chicken & Piccalilli Squares

MAKES

25

TIME

Prep: 45 minutes
Cook: 28 minutes

These square samosas are my favorite. Piccalilli, also called mustard pickle in the United States, is a relish with a spicy kick and a touch of sweetness, made with a mixture of vegetables. It tastes so good with the tender chicken wrapped in crispy, crunchy parcels. My mother-in-law made these one Ramadan, and at the first bite I knew I had to make them myself. These are easier to make than the traditional triangular samosas. Serve with Red Pepper Chutney (page 137) for dipping.

Ingredients

4 tablespoons (½ stick) butter
1 teaspoon cumin seeds
2 onions, finely chopped
1.1 pounds chicken breast, cut into ½-inch cubes
1 tablespoon garlic paste
1 tablespoon green chili paste
1 large potato, peeled and cut into ½-inch cubes
5 tablespoons piccalilli (mustard pickle)
5 tablespoons chili crisp
½ teaspoon salt
0.2 ounce fresh cilantro, finely chopped
2 tablespoons all-purpose flour
8 tablespoons water
1 package spring roll wrappers
oil, for deep-frying

Method

Melt the butter in a saucepan over low heat and sprinkle in the cumin seeds. When they start to sizzle, add the onions and fry for 5 minutes until soft and translucent.

Add the chicken, stir well, cover, and cook over medium heat for 25 minutes, or until very little moisture is left. Add the garlic paste and chili paste.

Meanwhile, boil the potatoes for 8–10 minutes until only just tender, then drain in a colander and set aside. Blitz the piccalilli in a food processor until smooth.

Add the potatoes, piccalilli, chili crisp, and salt to the chicken and mix everything together. Remove from the heat and set aside to cool completely, then stir in the chopped cilantro.

Make a paste by mixing the flour and water in a small bowl to a smooth consistency.

Take one of the spring roll wrappers and cut into long strips about 2 inches wide. Keep the wrappers you aren't using covered with a damp towel to keep them from drying out. Working with 2 strips at a time, follow the diagram on page 30 and place 1 strip on a clean work surface with one of the short edges toward you. Brush the bottom 2 inches of the strip with a little flour paste. Create an L shape by placing one end of the second strip on top of the flour paste at a 90-degree angle and press together.

Spoon 1½ tablespoons of the filling on the square section where the strips overlap. Fold the vertical strip down over the filling, then brush the top section that covers the filling with flour paste. Fold the second strip up and over the filling and press down to seal. Turn the parcel over and repeat the process, brushing with paste and folding until you have a square samosa. Repeat to make more squares until you've used up all the filling.

Heat the oil for deep-frying in a large saucepan over medium-high heat until it reaches 350°F. Fry the squares in batches for 3 minutes on each side until golden brown all over, then drain on paper towels. These are best eaten fresh on the day they are cooked.

 These chicken squares can be made in large batches and kept in the freezer. Arrange the uncooked squares on a baking sheet, then freeze until hard. Store in plastic bags in small quantities, then defrost and fry when required.

How to Fold a Samosa

The folding techniques for squares and samosas can seem tricky at first, but hopefully these drawings will help if you've not tried it before. Practice makes perfect!

 Squares

1.

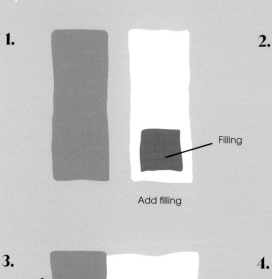

Filling

Add filling

2.

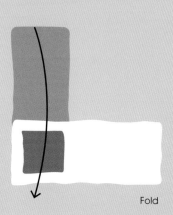

Fold

3.

Fold

4.

Flip over

5.

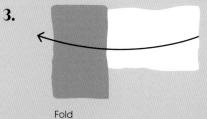

Fold and paste

6.

Samosas

1.

Fold

2. Fold

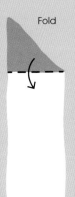

3.

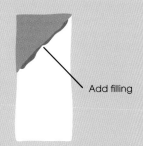

Add filling

4.

Fold and paste

5.

Fold and paste

6.

 Tortilla Samosas

1.

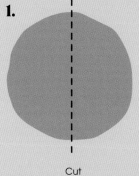

Cut

2.

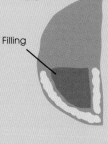

Filling

Add filling
and paste

3.

Fold

4.

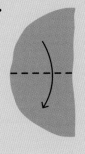

Jalapeño & Chicken Samosas

MAKES
25–30

TIME
Prep: 45 minutes
Cook: 36 minutes

One of my personal favorite savory snacks, and one we make every Ramadan. The filling is different from a traditional samosa, but I can assure you that from the first bite, you will be eagerly awaiting the next. Serve with Red Pepper Chutney (page 137) or Pineapple Chutney (page 136).

Ingredients

2 tablespoons oil, plus extra for deep-frying
1 onion, finely diced
1.1 pounds chicken breast, cut into small pieces
1 teaspoon ginger paste
1 teaspoon garlic paste
1 teaspoon ground black pepper
1 teaspoon ground cumin
1 teaspoon chili paste
½ red pepper, diced
½ green pepper, diced
4 tablespoons jalapeño sauce
4 ounces Cheddar, grated
7 ounces cream cheese, softened
0.5 ounce fresh cilantro, chopped
2 tablespoons spring onions, chopped
2 tablespoons all-purpose flour
8 tablespoons water
25–30 samosa leaves
3–4 eggs, beaten
9 ounces store-bought toasted bread crumbs
salt

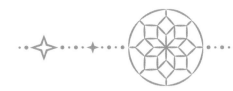

Method

Heat the 2 tablespoons of oil in a medium saucepan over low heat, add the onion, and cook for 5–6 minutes until soft and translucent. Add the chicken, cover, and cook for 25 minutes until the liquid released from the chicken has evaporated. Add the ginger paste, garlic paste, black pepper, cumin, chili paste, red and green peppers, and jalapeño sauce. Season with salt and cook for 5–6 minutes until the peppers have just softened. Remove from the heat and set aside to cool.

When the filling mixture has cooled down, add the grated Cheddar, cream cheese, fresh cilantro, and spring onions and stir everything together.

Make a paste by mixing the flour and water in a small bowl to a smooth consistency.

Lay a samosa leaf on a work surface with one short end facing you and fold according to the illustrations on page 31 to form a triangular pocket at the top. Fill the pocket with 1 teaspoon of filling, then use a pastry brush to brush some of the flour paste on the top of the filled triangle. Continue to wrap the samosa, brushing paste between the layers, to make a neat triangular parcel. Repeat with the remaining samosa leaves and filling.

Place the beaten egg in one bowl and the bread crumbs in a second shallow bowl. Dip the samosas in the egg, then coat with bread crumbs.

Heat the oil for deep-frying in a large saucepan over medium-high heat until it reaches 350°F. Drop a breadcrumb in the oil—if it sizzles, the oil is ready. Fry the samosas in batches for 2–3 minutes on each side until golden brown, then drain in a colander to remove excess oil. These are best eaten fresh on the day they are cooked.

 These samosas can be made in large batches and kept in the freezer. Arrange the coated samosas on a baking sheet, then freeze until hard. Store in plastic bags in small quantities, then defrost and fry when required.

Chicken Croquettes

| MAKES ABOUT **18** | TIME **Prep: 30 minutes** **Cook: 5 minutes** |

Chicken croquettes are absolutely amazing—creamy, minty, and spicy, these chicken nugget–style snacks are dipped in bread crumbs and deep fried until golden brown. When I was growing up, these were always my favorite, and it's the same with our kids! My mum would prepare these for Ramadan and make sure we had enough stocked in the freezer to last us throughout the month. These are super-easy and scrumptious.

Ingredients

1.1 pounds chicken breast, cut into 1½-inch chunks
½ cup heavy whipping cream
2 teaspoons garlic paste
½ teaspoon salt
½ teaspoon ground black pepper
1 teaspoon ground cumin
6–7 fresh chilies
1 ounce fresh mint leaves
1 ounce fresh cilantro
7 ounces store-bought toasted bread crumbs
oil, for deep-frying

Method

Place the chicken with the cream, garlic paste, salt, pepper, cumin, chilies, mint, and cilantro together in a food processor and blitz until very finely chopped. Shape into croquettes about 2 inches long and then leave on a plate, covered, to marinate in the fridge for 2 hours or overnight if possible.

Place the bread crumbs in a shallow bowl and turn the chunks of chicken in the crumbs to coat.

Heat the oil for deep-frying in a large saucepan over medium-high heat until it reaches 350°F. Fry the chicken pieces in batches for 4–5 minutes until golden brown all over, turning occasionally, then drain on paper towels.

 These chicken croquettes can be made in large batches and kept in the freezer. Cover the chicken pieces in bread crumbs and arrange on a baking sheet, then freeze until hard. Store in plastic bags in small quantities, then defrost and fry when required.

Keema Pies

MAKES
15

TIME
**Prep: 20 minutes
Cook: 25 minutes**

Golden brown, flaky puff pastry outside and deliciously spicy, succulent lamb inside. My children absolutely love pies, which are very popular in most households during Ramadan. I prepare them in batches a month ahead of time and keep them in the freezer, ready for Ramadan. I make these outside of Ramadan, too, because we love them that much. No matter how many I make, it's never enough and the moment they're baked they get snapped up. Serve with chutney, such as the Red Pepper Chutney (page 137).

Ingredients

2 tablespoons oil
1 teaspoon cumin seeds
1 onion, diced
14 ounces ground lamb
1 teaspoon ginger paste
1 teaspoon garlic paste
1 teaspoon green chili paste
1 teaspoon peri-peri seasoning
1 teaspoon ground cumin
1 teaspoon ground coriander
1 teaspoon ground black pepper
½ teaspoon salt
½ teaspoon garam masala
2 tablespoons diced red pepper
2 tablespoons diced green pepper
1 ounce frozen peas
0.2 ounce fresh cilantro leaves, finely chopped
2 spring onions, finely chopped
2 tablespoons all-purpose flour, plus extra for dusting
8 tablespoons water
2 x 11.3-ounce packages ready-rolled puff pastry
1 egg, beaten
sesame seeds, for sprinkling

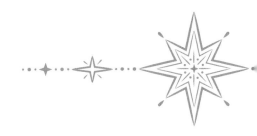

Method

Heat the oil in a wok over low heat and sprinkle in the cumin seeds. When they start to sizzle, add the onions and fry for 5 minutes until soft and translucent. Add the ground lamb and cook over medium heat for 10–15 minutes, stirring occasionally, until the meat is browned and only a little moisture remains.

Add the ginger paste, garlic paste, chili paste, peri-peri, cumin, ground coriander, black pepper, salt, garam masala, red and green peppers, and peas. Stir and cook for about 1 minute, then remove from the heat and set aside to cool. Stir in the chopped cilantro and spring onions.

Make a paste by mixing the flour and water in a small bowl to a smooth consistency. Preheat the oven to 375°F and line a baking sheet with parchment paper.

Unroll the puff pastry on a floured surface and cut out 15 squares about 4 inches across. Brush the edges of the squares with the flour paste and place a heaping tablespoon of the lamb mixture in the middle of each. Fold the pastry squares into triangles or rectangles—whichever shape you prefer—enclosing the filling and pressing the edges together gently to seal the parcels. Cut 2 small slits in the tops of the parcels to allow hot air to escape while they are baking.

Place the parcels on the prepared baking sheet, brush with beaten egg, and sprinkle with sesame seeds. Cook in the oven for 25 minutes until golden brown. Delish! These are best eaten fresh on the day they are cooked.

 TIP These keema pies can be made in large batches and kept in the freezer. Arrange the uncooked pies on a baking sheet, then freeze until hard. Store in plastic bags in small quantities, then defrost and bake when required.

Dynamite Prawns

Prawns are always a hit with my family, and the Dynamite variety are no exception. Saucy, spicy, and bite-sized, these are super addictive and will keep you going until the main meal arrives.

Ingredients

11 ounces raw king prawns, peeled and deveined
1 tablespoon dark soy sauce
1 teaspoon garlic powder
1 teaspoon ground white pepper
1 egg, beaten
2 tablespoons cornstarch
1½ cups all-purpose flour
1 teaspoon paprika
salt
oil, for deep-frying

SPICY MAYO SAUCE
5 ounces mayonnaise
2 ounces sriracha sauce
1.5 ounces sweet chili sauce
½ teaspoon chili powder

TO SERVE
green salad
finely chopped spring onion
lemon wedges

Method

For the sauce, place all the ingredients in a bowl, stir to combine, and set aside.

Place the prawns in another bowl with the soy sauce, garlic powder, white pepper, and egg and season with salt. Toss well to coat the prawns.

Place the cornstarch, all-purpose flour, and paprika on a plate and stir together. Coat the prawns thoroughly in the flour one at a time and place them on a plate ready for deep-frying.

Heat the oil for deep-frying in a large saucepan over medium-high heat until it reaches 350°F. Fry the prawns in batches for 3–4 minutes, flipping them over halfway through so they're evenly crisp and golden brown. Remove from the oil and drain on paper towels. Make sure not to overcook the prawns; otherwise, they will become chewy.

Place the crispy prawns in a bowl and add as much of the sauce as you like, completely coating them if you want. If you have remaining sauce, you can use it for dipping. Serve the prawns on a bed of green salad sprinkled with spring onions, with lemon wedges for squeezing.

Lamb & Mint Buns

MAKES
14

TIME
Prep: 30 minutes
Rising: 1 hour
Cook: 25 minutes

These soft and fluffy golden buns are stuffed with spiced, minty ground lamb. They are so filling and perfect for iftar, when breaking your fast. Great for bag lunches and days out too!

Ingredients

4 cups all-purpose flour
½ teaspoon salt
2 tablespoons sugar
2¼ teaspoons dried yeast
2 tablespoons powdered milk
½ cup milk
⅔ cup water
2 tablespoons butter
1 egg, beaten
1 tablespoon heavy cream
sesame seeds, for sprinkling

FILLING

1.1 pounds ground lamb
½ teaspoon cumin seeds
1 teaspoon ground black pepper
1 teaspoon ginger paste
1 teaspoon garlic paste
1 tablespoon oil
1 teaspoon ground cumin
1 teaspoon ground coriander
1 teaspoon chili powder
½ teaspoon garam masala
½ teaspoon salt
2 tablespoons finely chopped spring onion
0.2 ounce fresh cilantro, finely chopped
0.2 ounce fresh mint leaves, finely chopped

Method

Place the flour, salt, sugar, yeast, and milk powder in a large bowl. Place the milk, water, and butter in a small saucepan over low heat until just warm, then gradually add as much of the mixture as required to the flour to make a soft dough.

With lightly oiled hands, knead the dough until smooth, then form into a ball, return to the bowl, and cover with a cloth. Leave to rise for about 40 minutes, or until doubled in size.

For the filling, place the ground lamb in a saucepan over medium heat with the cumin seeds, black pepper, ginger paste, and garlic paste. Cook for about 10 minutes, stirring occasionally, then cover and continue cooking until only a little moisture remains. Add the oil, ground cumin, ground coriander, chili powder, garam masala, salt, spring onion, fresh cilantro, and mint.

Knock back the dough and knead lightly again, then divide into 14 pieces and roll into balls about 3 inches across. Make an indent in the middle of each ball, spoon in about 1 tablespoon of the filling, then carefully bring the dough back over the filling to enclose it. Roll each into a ball again, making sure the filling doesn't come out. Arrange on a baking sheet lined with parchment paper and allow to rise for 20 minutes. Preheat the oven to 350°F.

Whisk the beaten egg and cream together in a small bowl and use a pastry brush to brush the mixture on top of each bun. Sprinkle with sesame seeds. Cook in the oven for 25 minutes, or until golden brown. These are best eaten fresh on the day they are cooked.

 You can also make these delicious buns with ground beef or chicken.

 These buns can be made in large batches and kept in the freezer. Arrange the uncooked buns on a baking sheet, then freeze until hard. Store in plastic bags in small quantities, then defrost and bake when required.

Hariyali Chicken

SERVES

3

TIME

Prep: 30 minutes
Marinating: 2–3 hrs
Cook: 25 minutes

Also known as Hariyali Tikka or Green Chicken Tikka, this North Indian appetizer is easy to make yet delicious. The chicken pieces are marinated in a vibrant paste prepared with fresh herbs and green chilies—it's the color of this paste that gives the dish its name.

Ingredients

0.5 ounce fresh mint leaves
0.5 ounce fresh cilantro
1 ounce fresh ginger, peeled
2 garlic cloves
4–5 fresh green chilies
14 ounces boneless chicken thighs or breast, cut into 1-inch chunks
3 tablespoons oil, plus extra for greasing
1 teaspoon ground cumin
1 teaspoon ground coriander
1 teaspoon mango powder
½ teaspoon ground turmeric
½ teaspoon ground black pepper
1 teaspoon salt
2 ounces plain yogurt
2 tablespoons lemon juice

Method

Place the mint leaves, fresh cilantro, ginger, garlic, and green chilies in a food processor and blend until smooth. Transfer to a bowl with all the remaining ingredients—at this point, your kitchen will be smelling absolutely fresh, lemony, and minty. Mix well to coat each piece of chicken and place in the fridge to marinate for 2–3 hours or, better, overnight.

Preheat the oven to 350°F, line a baking sheet with foil, and grease it lightly. Soak some bamboo skewers in water for 30 minutes—this way they do not burn during cooking. Thread the marinated chicken pieces on the skewers and place on the prepared baking sheet. Cook in the oven for 25 minutes, or until the chicken is cooked through.

 Serve salad and the Mint & Cilantro Yogurt Chutney on page 137 with these skewers.

Crispy Pakoras

MAKES ABOUT **15**

TIME
Prep: 25 minutes
Cook: 3 minutes

The humble pakora—these crispy, deep-fried snacks really don't need an introduction. Basic pakoras are made with sliced onions, fresh fenugreek leaves, chickpea flour, and Indian spices, but you can add other vegetables, such as grated carrots and potatoes, or even chicken. My dad absolutely loves them (these and a bowl of warm custard), so I'm always sure to keep some ready when he visits. Serve them fresh and hot—you will soon see them disappearing one by one from the plate—accompanied by my Tomato & Cilantro Chutney (page 133).

Ingredients

1 large onion, finely chopped
1 large red onion, finely chopped
4 ounces spinach, finely chopped
4 ounces fresh fenugreek leaves, chopped (stems removed)
½ teaspoon ground turmeric
½ teaspoon chili powder
1 teaspoon ground coriander
1 teaspoon ground cumin
¼ teaspoon carom seeds (ajwain)
2 teaspoons garlic paste
2 teaspoons green chili paste
1 tablespoon dried fenugreek leaves
1 heaping tablespoon rice flour
½ teaspoon baking powder
7 ounces chickpea flour
7 ounces canned corn
about 1 cup water
salt
oil, for deep-frying

Method

Place the onions in a large bowl with the chopped spinach and fresh fenugreek. Add the turmeric, chili powder, ground coriander, cumin, carom seeds, garlic paste, chili paste, dried fenugreek, rice flour, baking powder, and chickpea flour. Season with salt.

Add the corn and the liquid from the can—just enough water to hold the mixture together—the consistency shouldn't be too thick or too thin.

Heat the oil for deep-frying in a large saucepan over medium-high heat until it reaches 350°F. Drop a little bit of the mixture into the oil—if it sizzles, the oil is ready. Drop heaping tablespoons of the mixture into the oil in batches and cook for 2–3 minutes until golden brown and crispy all over, turning occasionally, then drain on paper towels. These pakoras are best eaten hot and fresh on the day they are cooked.

Salmon Pakoras

MAKES ABOUT **10**

TIME
Prep: 10 minutes
Cook: 4 minutes

This delicious deep-fried starter is so addictive. The fish is lightly spiced with aromatic spices and herbs, and the seasoned batter makes it so crispy, flavorful, and tasty.

Ingredients

9 ounces boneless, skinless salmon, cut into chunks
1 teaspoon chopped garlic
1 teaspoon paprika
1 teaspoon ground black pepper
2 tablespoons lemon juice
1 tablespoon chopped fresh dill
salt
oil, for deep-frying

BATTER
3 tablespoons chickpea flour
1 tablespoon cornstarch
½ teaspoon chili powder
½ teaspoon nigella seeds
½ teaspoon salt
½ teaspoon ground black pepper
½ cup water

Method

Place the salmon in a bowl with the garlic, paprika, black pepper, lemon juice, and dill and season with salt. Leave to marinate in the fridge for 30 minutes.

For the batter, place the chickpea flour in a bowl with the cornstarch, chili powder, nigella seeds, salt, and black pepper. Add the water bit by bit, stirring all the time to make a smooth batter—it should be thick enough to coat the salmon pieces.

Heat the oil for deep-frying in a large saucepan over medium-high heat until it reaches 350°F. Drop a little bit of the batter into the oil—if it sizzles, the oil is ready. Dip the salmon pieces in the batter, then carefully drop into the oil in batches and cook for about 2 minutes on each side until golden brown. Drain on paper towels.

Chinese-Style Spring Rolls

MAKES
20

TIME
Prep: 30 minutes
Cook: 10 minutes

These flaky, crispy spring rolls are filled with a mixture of crunchy vegetables and intriguing Chinese-inspired flavors. Spring rolls are popular appetizers. They are so easy to make with readily available spring roll wrappers and even easier to eat—one will definitely not be enough. If you like to dip, serve them with Red Pepper Chutney (page 137) or sweet chili sauce.

Ingredients

1 nest of dried rice noodles
1 tablespoon oil, plus extra for deep-frying
1 onion, finely sliced
4 ounces white cabbage, shredded
1 carrot, peeled and julienned
2 tablespoons dark soy sauce
3 tablespoons sweet chili sauce
1 teaspoon chili flakes
2 tablespoons diced red pepper
2 tablespoons diced green pepper
2 tablespoons chopped fresh cilantro
1 spring onion, chopped
1 tablespoon sesame seeds
2 tablespoons all-purpose flour
8 tablespoons water
20 spring roll wrappers, about 6-inch square
salt

 TIP These spring rolls can be made in large batches and kept in the freezer. Arrange the uncooked rolls on a baking sheet, then freeze until hard. Store in plastic bags in small quantities, then defrost and fry when required.

Method

Soak the noodles in cold water according to package instructions until soft, then drain in a colander.

Heat the oil in a wok over high heat and add the onion, cabbage, and carrot. Cover the wok and cook for 2–4 minutes until the cabbage has wilted slightly. Add the soy sauce, sweet chili sauce, and chili flakes and season with salt.

Add the drained noodles, peppers, fresh cilantro, spring onion, and sesame seeds, tossing well to ensure everything is evenly coated, and stir-fry for 2 minutes. Leave the mixture to cool completely.

Make a paste by mixing the flour and water in a small bowl to a smooth consistency.

Place one of the spring roll wrappers on a flat surface with a corner facing toward you. Arrange 2 tablespoons of the filling in a line across the wrapper about 2 inches up from the corner that is closest to you. Roll the bottom corner over the filling, then fold in both sides of the wrapper. Continue rolling away from you until you have a neat cigar shape. Use a pastry brush to brush a little of the flour paste under the corner of the wrapper to seal it.

Heat the oil for deep-frying in a large saucepan over medium-high heat until it reaches 350°F. Fry the spring rolls in batches for 3 minutes on each side until golden brown, then drain on paper towels. These are best eaten fresh on the day they are cooked.

Veggie Pizza Pinwheels

MAKES
12

TIME
Prep: 35 minutes
Cook: 15 minutes

Puff pastry pinwheels are one of the easiest treats to make—using store-bought puff pastry, of course. Lightly spiced and filled with red onions, mixed peppers, olives, and cheese, these are extremely addictive. Serve with Tomato & Cilantro Chutney (page 133).

Ingredients

2 tablespoons chopped black olives
2 tablespoons chopped red pepper
2 tablespoons chopped green pepper
2 tablespoons canned corn, drained
1 small red onion, diced
1 teaspoon dried mixed herbs
1 teaspoon chili flakes
½ teaspoon ground black pepper
4 ounces medium Cheddar, grated
13 ounces ready-rolled puff pastry
6 tablespoons ready-made smooth tomato
    pasta sauce
1 egg, beaten
salt

Method

Place the olives in a bowl with the red and green peppers, corn, red onion, mixed herbs, chili flakes, black pepper, and grated Cheddar and season with salt. Toss everything together.

Unroll the puff pastry and spread a layer of pasta sauce over it, leaving a ½-inch border around the edges. Scatter the veggie mix evenly on top. Roll up the pastry lengthwise to make a tight roll and chill in the fridge for 10 minutes. Preheat the oven to 350°F and line a baking sheet with parchment paper.

Use a sharp knife to cut the roll into 12 equal slices and arrange them on the prepared baking sheet. Brush each pinwheel lightly with beaten egg and cook in the oven for 12–15 minutes until puffed and golden brown. These are best eaten fresh from the oven.

 You can also use ready-rolled pizza dough—it will taste just as good!

 These pinwheels can be made in large batches and kept in the freezer. Arrange the uncooked pinwheels on a baking sheet, then freeze until hard. Store in plastic bags in small quantities, then defrost and bake when required.

Chicken Bread Rolls

MAKES
12

TIME
Prep: 30 minutes
Cook: 6 minutes

These are so awesome, you're going to love them, and I'm sure you'll agree they are super easy to make and so addictive. The cream cheese melts inside, making the filling lovely and saucy. These are very popular in Indian homes, served as a snack, at picnics, or when entertaining guests. Serve with Red Pepper Chutney (page 137).

Ingredients

4 tablespoons (½ stick) butter
1 onion, finely diced
11 ounces chicken breast, cut into ½-inch cubes
1 teaspoon ginger paste
1 teaspoon garlic paste
1 teaspoon green chili paste
3 ounces canned corn, drained
½ red pepper, finely diced
½ green pepper, finely diced
1 teaspoon ground cumin
1 teaspoon ground black pepper
11 ounces cream cheese, softened
0.2 ounce fresh cilantro, finely chopped
12 slices of white bread
2 tablespoons all-purpose flour
8 tablespoons water
2 eggs, beaten
6 ounces store-bought toasted bread crumbs
salt
oil, for deep-frying

Method

Heat the butter in a large frying pan over medium-low heat, add the onion, and fry for 5 minutes until soft and translucent. Add the chicken, ginger paste, garlic paste, and chili paste and cook for 20 minutes, stirring occasionally, until the liquid from the chicken has nearly evaporated and only a small amount of moisture is left.

Add the corn, red and green peppers, cumin, and black pepper and season with salt. Give the mixture a good stir, remove from the heat, and set aside to cool completely. Once cool, stir in the softened cream cheese and fresh cilantro.

Warm the slices of bread in batches in the microwave for 40 seconds, then cut off and discard the crusts. Use a rolling pin to roll out the slices to about ¼ inch thick. Make a paste by mixing the flour and water in a small bowl to a smooth consistency. Use a pastry brush to brush the edges of the bread slices with the flour paste.

To assemble, place 2 tablespoons of the filling along one short end of a slice of bread and roll tightly into a cigar shape. Pinch the ends of the roll to seal and repeat with the remaining bread and filling. Place the beaten egg in one bowl and the bread crumbs in a second shallow bowl. Dip the rolls in the egg, then coat with bread crumbs.

Heat the oil for deep-frying in a large saucepan over medium-high heat until it reaches 350°F. Fry the rolls in batches for 3 minutes on each side until golden brown, then drain on paper towels. These are best eaten fresh on the day they are cooked.

 TIP These bread rolls can be made in large batches and kept in the freezer. Arrange the coated rolls on a baking sheet, then freeze until hard. Store in plastic bags in small quantities, then defrost and fry when required.

COMFORTING
Classics

For me, the recipes in this chapter hold deep fond memories of happy times with family, moments of caring, love, and fun. My Comforting Classics will truly feed your soul—I'm sure you will enjoy them as much as we do.

Lamb Haleem

SERVES
6

TIME
Prep: 40 mins plus overnight soaking
Cook: 2 hrs 15 mins

(If you have a pressure cooker, this will cut your cooking time in half)

Perfect to enjoy at the end of a fasting day, haleem is a comforting and hearty dish with succulent, melt-in-the-mouth lamb. The finished dish is somewhere between a stew and a soup. Serve with Naan (pages 130–1) or enjoy just on its own.

Ingredients

5 ounces broth mix
2.2 pounds diced lamb shoulder or leg
about 5 cups water
4 tablespoons basmati rice
½ cup oil
1 tablespoon ghee
1 teaspoon cumin seeds
2 cinnamon sticks
5–6 black peppercorns
5–6 cloves
5–6 cardamom pods
2 bay leaves
2 large onions, finely chopped
1 fresh tomato, diced
1 tablespoon green chili paste
1½ tablespoons ginger paste
1½ tablespoons garlic paste
1 tablespoon ground cumin
1 tablespoon ground coriander
½ teaspoon ground turmeric
0.5 ounce fresh cilantro
0.5 ounce fresh mint leaves
¼ teaspoon garam masala
salt

GARNISH

finely chopped fresh cilantro
finely chopped fresh mint
1 ounce fresh ginger, peeled and julienned
1 fresh red chili, sliced
3 tablespoons store-bought fried onions
1 lemon, cut into wedges

Method

Place the broth mix in a large bowl, cover with cold water, and leave to soak overnight.

Heat a large wide saucepan over low heat. Place the lamb in the saucepan and boil off the liquid that is released from the meat, stirring occasionally to make sure the meat doesn't burn. This will take 20–25 minutes. Add the water, rice, and broth mix and simmer over low heat for 1 hour, stirring occasionally, until the rice is soft and the mixture is nice and thick.

Pour the oil into another large pan over medium-low heat, add the ghee, cumin seeds, cinnamon sticks, peppercorns, cloves, cardamom pods, bay leaves, and the onions and fry for 20 minutes until golden brown. Add the tomato, green chili paste, ginger and garlic paste, cumin, ground coriander, turmeric, and salt and stir together over low heat until the spices are well combined.

Add the onion and tomato mixture to the meat saucepan and mix everything together. Blitz together the cilantro and mint leaves in a food processor or chop them very finely and add to the haleem with the garam masala to enhance the flavor. Season with salt.

Serve in bowls, garnished with chopped cilantro and mint, fresh ginger, chilies, and fried onions. Squeeze some lemon juice on top to taste.

 TIP If the haleem is too thick, you can thin it by adding some extra water.

Khuri & Khitchri

This classic dish of spicy yogurt curry and yellow rice goes perfectly with Bombay Potatoes (page 62) or Spinach, Potatoes & Peas (page 59). Don't forget the poppadoms on the side.

Ingredients

KHITCHRI

1 tablespoon oil
1 tablespoon ghee, plus extra for finishing
1 teaspoon cumin seeds
1 onion, finely sliced
1 cinnamon stick
3–4 black peppercorns
3–4 cloves
3–4 cardamom pods
2–3 star anise
1 bay leaf
2½ cups water
½ teaspoon ground turmeric
1 teaspoon salt
4 ounces toor dhal (split pigeon peas)
9 ounces basmati rice

KHURI

1 tablespoon ghee
1 tablespoon oil
1 small onion, diced
1 small fresh tomato, diced
1 teaspoon cumin seeds
1 teaspoon ground coriander
¼ teaspoon ground turmeric
1 teaspoon ginger paste
1 teaspoon garlic paste
2 teaspoons green chili paste
1.1 pounds plain yogurt
½ cup single cream
½ cup whole milk
¼ cup water
1 tablespoon chickpea flour

GARNISH

1 teaspoon cumin seeds
1 tablespoon ghee
6–7 curry leaves
0.5 ounce fresh cilantro, finely chopped

Method

For the khitchri, heat a large saucepan over medium-low heat and add the oil, ghee, cumin seeds, sliced onion, cinnamon stick, peppercorns, cloves, cardamom pods, star anise, and bay leaf. Fry gently for 10 minutes until lightly golden brown. Add the water, turmeric, and salt and bring to a boil.

Wash the toor dhal and rice in a sieve under cold running water until the water runs clear. Once the water in the saucepan starts to bubble, add the toor dhal and rice, stir, and partially cover the pan with a lid (not completely or the water may boil over). Cook over medium heat for 15 minutes until the water has been absorbed, then give it a stir once without disturbing the rice too much. Cover fully with the lid and cook for another 15 minutes over low heat—with the buildup of steam, the rice will fully cook and fluff up. Finish with a little ghee on top for that extra buttery flavor.

For the khuri, heat a saucepan over medium heat and add the ghee, oil, onion, tomato, cumin seeds, ground coriander, turmeric, ginger paste, garlic paste, and chili paste. Season with salt and cook for about 3–4 minutes until the tomato and onion have softened.

Whisk the yogurt together with the cream, milk, water, and chickpea flour. Pour into the masala mixture and whisk together over low heat for about 1 minute until hot, making sure not to curdle the khuri. If you want a thinner consistency, add a little more water.

For the garnish, heat a small frying pan over medium heat and dry-fry the cumin seeds for 1 minute until they turn dark brown in color. Add the ghee and it will start to sizzle. Throw in the curry leaves and fresh cilantro and stir together for about 30 seconds over low heat. Pour the mixture on top of the khuri.

Dish up a portion of khitchri, then pour as much khuri on top as you like.

Spinach, Potatoes & Peas

I absolutely love fresh spinach, so tender and sweet. You really have to try this—it's very easy to make and on your table in less than 30 minutes. This dish is the perfect accompaniment to Khuri & Khitchri (pages 56–7), but it's also delicious served simply with Roti (pages 126–7).

Ingredients

4 ounces frozen peas
2 tablespoons oil
1 onion, finely sliced
1 teaspoon ginger paste
1 teaspoon garlic paste
1 teaspoon green chili paste
1 potato, cubed
1 teaspoon ground cumin
1 teaspoon ground coriander
½ teaspoon ground turmeric
1 fresh tomato, diced
1.1 pounds spinach, finely chopped
salt

Method

Cook the frozen peas in a saucepan of boiling water for 3–4 minutes, then drain in a colander.

Heat a medium saucepan over low heat, add the oil and onion and cook for about 2 minutes until softened. Add the ginger paste, garlic paste, and chili paste and cook, stirring, for another minute.

Add the potato, stir well, cover, and cook for 10 minutes, or until the potato has softened. (If the saucepan is looking a bit dry, add a splash of water to the potato to help it cook. Sometimes the steam created is enough, but if needed, add some additional water.)

Once the potato is cooked, add the cumin, coriander, turmeric, tomato, spinach, and peas and season with salt. Stir everything together, cover, and cook over medium heat for 8–10 minutes until the tomatoes have softened and the spinach has wilted.

Sizzling Lamb Steaks

SERVES

4

TIME

Prep: 15 minutes
Marinating: 2–3 hrs
Cook: 16 minutes

My sizzling lamb steaks are perfect for the end of a day of fasting. Cooked in a frying pan, they are loaded with flavors, including herbs and Worcestershire sauce, and take literally minutes to cook. Great served with salad and chips.

Ingredients

2 tablespoons olive oil
1 tablespoon Worcestershire sauce
2 tablespoons chili sauce
1 teaspoon chili powder
1 tablespoon ground black pepper
1 teaspoon dried oregano
2 tablespoons lemon juice
4 lean lamb steaks
2 tablespoons oil
salt

Method

Mix the olive oil, Worcestershire sauce, chili sauce, chili powder, black pepper, oregano, and lemon juice in a bowl. Add the lamb steaks, mix well to make sure they are completely coated, and marinate in the fridge for 2–3 hours.

Heat a frying pan or griddle pan over medium heat, add the oil, and cook the steaks for 2–3 minutes on each side for medium-rare, or 6–8 minutes on each side for medium to well done. Season with salt and serve.

Bombay Potatoes

SERVES
3–4

TIME
Prep: 15 minutes
Cook: 25 minutes

This very traditional, classic, and versatile side dish can be enjoyed with so many main meals, although it's normally served alongside Khuri & Khitchri (pages 56–7). My family also loves this on its own with Roti (pages 126–7) or as a Sunday morning brunch with eggs. It's so simple to make with just a handful of ingredients, yet ever so comforting, warming, and satisfying.

Ingredients

2 large potatoes, peeled and cut into ¼-inch slices
1 teaspoon ground turmeric
1 teaspoon ground cumin
1 teaspoon ground coriander
1 teaspoon chili powder
1 teaspoon ginger paste
1 teaspoon garlic paste
2 tablespoons oil
salt
chopped fresh cilantro, to garnish

Method

Place the potato slices in a large bowl with the turmeric, cumin, ground coriander, chili powder, ginger paste, and garlic paste. Season with salt and mix everything together with a spoon or your hands to coat the potato slices with the spices.

Heat the oil in a frying pan over medium-low heat heat and add the potatoes. Stir, cover, and cook for 15 minutes, or until the potatoes are cooked through, stirring occasionally so they don't stick to the pan. Garnish with fresh cilantro.

 TIP Any leftover potatoes can make a quick lunch. Place some potato slices in the middle of a roti, add some ketchup, and roll up. It tastes so good!

Creamy Mixed Vegetables

SERVES
2–3

TIME
Prep: 20 minutes
Cook: 10 minutes

This simple dish is so easy to prepare and so delicious—sure to pamper your palate. Serve with Sizzling Lamb Steaks (page 61), Masala Roast Chicken (page 72), or just on its own.

Ingredients

1 large potato, peeled and cut into 1-inch chunks
1 sweet potato, peeled and cut into 1-inch chunks
1 large carrot, peeled and cut into 1-inch chunks
1 ear corn on the cob, cut into 3 pieces
2 ounces frozen peas
3 tablespoons butter
1 teaspoon garlic paste
3 tablespoons brown sugar
1 teaspoon ground black pepper
1 tablespoon chili flakes
1 teaspoon dried mixed herbs
½ teaspoon salt
½ cup cream or heavy whipping cream

Method

Place the potato, sweet potato, carrot, corn, and peas in a steamer and cook for 20 minutes, or until just tender with a slight bite to them. Do not overcook or they will become mushy. Alternatively, cook the vegetables in a saucepan of boiling water if you prefer.

Melt the butter in a saucepan over low heat and add the garlic paste, sugar, black pepper, chili flakes, mixed herbs, salt, and cream. Gently simmer the sauce for 8–10 minutes until nice and creamy. Add the vegetables to the sauce and stir together.

 TIP Other vegetables also work well in this dish—try cauliflower, spring beans, and mixed peppers too!

Prawn Jalfrezi

SERVES
2–3

TIME
Prep: 20 minutes
Cook: 16 minutes

Typically made with chili, tomatoes, and onions among other ingredients, a jalfrezi is considered to be a hot and spicy thick sauce rather than a full-on curry. I guess you could call it an Indian stir-fry, and it's so easy to prepare and cook. Jalfrezi can be made with only vegetables, or with chicken too, but it's ever so quick with prawns. Serve with Naan (pages 130–1), Roti (pages 126–7), or Basmati Rice (page 132).

Ingredients

3 tablespoons oil
1 large onion, finely chopped
2 ounces canned chopped tomatoes
½ red pepper, cut into chunks
½ green pepper, cut into chunks
1 large red onion, cut into 1-inch chunks
1 teaspoon garlic paste
1 teaspoon chili flakes
1 teaspoon chili powder
1 teaspoon ground turmeric
1 teaspoon ground cumin
1.1 pounds raw king prawns, peeled
½ teaspoon salt
¼ cup water
1 teaspoon lemon juice

GARNISH
1 spring onion, finely chopped
fresh cilantro
sliced red chili

Method

Heat a wok over low heat, add the oil and chopped onion, and sauté for about 3 minutes until translucent. Blitz the tomatoes in a food processor until smooth, then add to the wok with the red and green peppers and red onion. Add the garlic paste, chili flakes, chili powder, turmeric, and cumin and cook the spices for about a minute.

Stir in the prawns, salt, water, and lemon juice, cover, and cook for 10–12 minutes until cooked through. Garnish with spring onion, cilantro, and red chili before serving.

 You can add extra vegetables to this tasty jalfrezi—stir in some chopped spinach or sweet potato chunks if you'd like to give it a veggie boost.

Butter Chicken

A royal dish if ever there was one, Butter Chicken is known for its luxuriously rich texture and for me, the thicker and creamier the better. It's a flavorful, aromatic curry with a butter and tomato base—wonderfully creamy and tastes out of this world. My children absolutely love this beautiful dish. I make this often and serve it with Basmati Rice (page 132). My husband loves Butter Chicken too and makes it using this recipe—I've got to say it's pretty good! Forget going out to dinner—make this and have a night in. You can thank me later!

Ingredients

4–5 tablespoons oil
2 bay leaves
1 onion, finely chopped
1.1 pounds chicken breast, cut into chunks
1 teaspoon ginger paste
1 teaspoon garlic paste
1 teaspoon chili powder
1 teaspoon chili flakes
1 tablespoon Kashmiri chili powder
1 teaspoon ground coriander
1 teaspoon ground cumin
½ teaspoon ground turmeric
1 tablespoon butter chicken masala or
      tandoori masala
½ teaspoon salt
½ teaspoon ground black pepper
1 tablespoon dried fenugreek leaves
1 fresh tomato, chopped
9 ounces tomato passata
½–⅔ cup water
½ cup milk
⅔ cup cream or heavy whipping cream
2 tablespoons butter
2 tablespoons lemon juice
chopped fresh cilantro, to garnish

Method

Heat the oil in a large saucepan over low heat, add the bay leaves and onion and cook for 5 minutes until golden brown. Add the chicken, ginger paste, and garlic paste and cook for 25 minutes until only a little moisture is left from the chicken.

Add the chili powder, chili flakes, Kashmiri chili powder, ground coriander, cumin, turmeric, butter chicken masala or tandoori masala, salt, pepper, and dried fenugreek and stir well. Add the fresh tomato and passata, cook for 1 minute, then pour in the water, milk, and cream and stir well. Simmer for 8–10 minutes until the sauce has thickened.

Add the butter, letting it melt through the sauce, then add the lemon juice and serve sprinkled with chopped cilantro.

Kidney Bean Curry

SERVES
4

TIME
Prep: 20 minutes
Cook: 50 minutes

A hearty, aromatic, protein-rich curry with fragrant spices, onions, and tomatoes, and one of my mother-in-law's specialities (hers is always so good). This is a staple dish in our home, and I'm sure it will become one of yours too! Serve with Basmati Rice (page 132) or Roti (see pages 126-7).

Ingredients

5 tablespoons oil
1 teaspoon cumin seeds
2 onions, finely chopped
6–7 curry leaves
14 ounces canned chopped tomatoes
1 teaspoon ground turmeric
1 teaspoon chili powder
1 tablespoon ground coriander
1 teaspoon ground cumin
1 teaspoon garlic paste
1 teaspoon ginger paste
1 teaspoon green chili paste
2 x 14-ounce cans kidney beans, drained
3⅓ cups water
salt

GARNISH
chopped fresh cilantro
pinch of garam masala

Method

Heat a large wide saucepan over medium-low heat and add the oil and cumin seeds. When they start to sizzle, add the onions and curry leaves and fry until the onions are golden brown.

Blitz the canned tomatoes in a food processor until smooth, then add to the saucepan with the turmeric, chili powder, ground coriander, cumin, garlic paste, ginger paste, and chili paste. Season with salt, stir, cover, and cook the masala over medium heat for 8–10 minutes until reduced. You want to really cook the spices nicely and cook off the rawness of the ginger and garlic.

Add the kidney beans and water and simmer for 25 minutes. While the curry is simmering, use the back of a spoon to crush some of the kidney beans—not all of them—into the sauce. This will thicken the curry and make it creamier. Serve garnished with fresh cilantro and a sprinkle of garam masala on top.

Chicken, Cassava & Corn Casserole

SERVES
6–7

TIME
Prep: 30 minutes
Cook: 2 hours

My grandmother introduced me to this tasty dish, and her mother showed her how to make it, a dish she used to make in Malawi. I would describe it as more of a stew than a curry. When you start making this recipe it's very similar to making a chicken curry, but the sweet and nutty cassava and the creamy coconut add a whole new level of deliciousness.

Ingredients

1.1 pounds frozen cassava
2 ears corn on the cob, cut into 1-inch pieces
3 tablespoons oil
1 onion, finely sliced
11 ounces chicken thighs on the bone
11 ounces chicken breast, cut into chunks
1 teaspoon ground turmeric
1 teaspoon chili powder
1 teaspoon chili flakes
1 tablespoon ground cumin
1 tablespoon ground coriander
1 tablespoon ginger paste
1 tablespoon garlic paste
1 teaspoon green chili paste
4 ounces canned chopped tomatoes
1 fresh tomato, finely chopped
7 ounces creamed coconut, chopped
2 cups water
salt
chopped fresh cilantro, to garnish

WHOLE SPICES
1 teaspoon cumin seeds
2 cinnamon sticks
3 cardamom pods
5–6 black peppercorns
5–6 cloves

Method

Place the cassava in a steamer and cook for 25 minutes, or until just tender with a slight bite to it, adding the corn after 5 minutes. Do not overcook or they will become mushy. Alternatively, cook the vegetables in a saucepan of boiling water if you prefer. Cut the cassava into 1-inch chunks and set aside.

Heat a large wide saucepan over medium-low heat and add the oil and the whole spices. When they start to sizzle, add the onion and fry for 15 minutes, or until golden brown. Add the chicken, turmeric, chili powder, chili flakes, cumin, ground coriander, ginger paste, garlic paste, and chili paste. Season with salt, stir, and cook for 30 minutes, stirring occasionally, until no moisture is left.

Blitz the canned tomatoes with the fresh tomato in a food processor until smooth, add to the chicken, and cook for 10–12 minutes. Add the cassava, corn, and creamed coconut and pour in the water. Stir well and simmer for 15 minutes until the casserole thickens. Serve into bowls, garnish with fresh cilantro, and enjoy!

Achari Kheema

SERVES
3–4

TIME
Prep: 20 minutes
Cook: 1 hr 5 mins

I absolutely love ground meat, whether it's chicken or lamb. Ground meat is so versatile—great for kebabs, rice dishes, and other savory dishes, too. Ground meat cooks very quickly, so when you don't have much time on your hands, try this delicious, spicy, and saucy dish. Your family will enjoy it for sure. Serve with Naan (pages 130–1) or Roti (pages 126–7).

Ingredients

4 tablespoons oil
1–2 bay leaves
1–2 cinnamon sticks
1 onion, diced
1 teaspoon ginger paste
1 teaspoon garlic paste
1.1 pounds ground lamb
1 teaspoon chili powder
1 teaspoon ground turmeric
1 teaspoon mango powder
1 teaspoon dried fenugreek leaves
1 ounce fresh fenugreek, finely chopped
1 tablespoon lemon juice
2 fresh tomatoes, finely chopped
2 tablespoons tomato purée
2 tablespoons plain yogurt
⅓ cup water
2 jalapeño chilies, halved
½ teaspoon nigella seeds
salt
finely chopped fresh cilantro, to garnish

WHOLE SPICES
3–4 dried chilies
2 teaspoons coriander seeds
1 teaspoon fennel seeds
1 teaspoon nigella seeds
3–4 cloves
5–6 black peppercorns
½ teaspoon cardamom seeds

Method

Heat a frying pan over medium heat and dry-fry the whole spices for 8 minutes, stirring, until fragrant. Put into a food processor, grind to a powder, and set aside.

Heat a medium saucepan over low heat and add the oil, bay leaves, and cinnamon sticks. Add the onion and fry for 4–5 minutes, or until golden brown. Add the spices you have ground, the ginger paste, and garlic paste and cook for 30 seconds. Add the ground lamb, stir well, cover, and cook until the lamb has changed color and the liquid has evaporated, about 25–30 minutes.

Add the chili powder, turmeric, mango powder, dried fenugreek, fresh fenugreek, lemon juice, tomatoes, tomato purée, yogurt, water, and jalapeños. Season with salt, stir everything together, and simmer over low heat for 15–20 minutes until the tomatoes have softened and broken down. Sprinkle with the nigella seeds and serve garnished with fresh cilantro.

Masala Roast Chicken & Herby Potatoes

SERVES
2

TIME
Prep: 40 minutes
Marinating: 1–2 hrs
Cook: 1 hr 10 mins

Indian-spiced roast chicken is juicy, delicious, and perfect for family dinners. You can roast, grill, or panfry the chicken as you prefer. Adjust the amount of chili powder to your liking.

Ingredients

4 chicken breasts, thighs, or drumsticks
½ cup oil, plus extra for drizzling
½ teaspoon ground turmeric
1 teaspoon chili powder
1 teaspoon ground black pepper
1 tablespoon ground coriander
1 tablespoon ground cumin
1 tablespoon hot paprika
1 tablespoon peri-peri seasoning
1 tablespoon ginger paste
1 tablespoon garlic paste
4 tablespoons lemon juice
½ teaspoon salt

HERBY POTATOES

1.1 pounds small new potatoes, halved
3 tablespoons butter
2 teaspoons fresh thyme leaves
2 teaspoons finely chopped fresh mint
2 teaspoons finely chopped fresh parsley
1 teaspoon ground black pepper
1 teaspoon salt

Method

Preheat the oven to 375°F. Cut a few deep slits into the chicken, then place the pieces in a bowl with all the remaining chicken ingredients and mix really well to coat the chicken, rubbing the spices into the slits. Leave in the fridge for 1–2 hours to marinate.

Line a roasting pan with foil and place the chicken in the pan. Drizzle with a little oil, cover with foil, and cook in the oven for 30–40 minutes, removing the foil halfway through. The chicken will release juices as it cooks—when the juices run clear, the chicken is done.

For the herby potatoes, boil the potatoes in a saucepan of water for 12–15 minutes, or until tender. Drain and return to the pan, then add the remaining potato ingredients and coat the potatoes in the buttery herb sauce.

FUSION

Flavors

With innovative and creative mixing of cultures and flavors, these vibrant and tasty dishes will tantalize your taste buds, sometimes spicy and sometimes tangy. These are very tasty dishes you will want to make again and again—be sure to make enough for the whole family.

Sweet & Sour Prawns

SERVES
2

TIME
Prep: 20 minutes
Cook: 20 minutes

Succulent king prawns tossed in a sweet and sour sauce—you really don't need any special ingredients for this recipe, and it is so easy to put together. Prawns really don't take long to cook, so it's the perfect quick recipe. This is definitely a winner in our household.

Ingredients

2 tablespoons cornstarch
2 tablespoons water
2 tablespoons dark soy sauce
1 tablespoon rice vinegar
2 tablespoons sugar
8 ounces canned pineapple chunks in juice
2 tablespoons sweet chili sauce
2 tablespoons sesame oil
2 garlic cloves, chopped
1 tablespoon chili flakes
1 onion, thinly sliced
½ red pepper, cut into chunks
½ green pepper, cut into chunks
10 ounces raw king prawns, peeled

GARNISH
1 spring onion, julienned
1 jalapeño, sliced (optional)

Method

Place the cornstarch and water in a medium bowl and mix to a paste. Add the soy sauce, rice vinegar, sugar, pineapple juice from the can, and sweet chili sauce and stir well to make a smooth sauce.

Heat a wok over medium heat. Add the oil, garlic, chili flakes, and onion and stir-fry for 5–6 minutes until lightly golden brown. Add the peppers and pineapple and stir-fry for 2–3 minutes over high heat. Pour in the sauce and cook for another 2 minutes.

Add the prawns, mix everything together, and stir-fry for 8 minutes over medium heat until the prawns are cooked through. Garnish with spring onion and sliced chili.

Chicken Chow Mein

SERVES

3–4

TIME

Prep: 15 minutes
Cook: 35 minutes

My children absolutely love noodles, and this is my go-to meal when I'm stuck for ideas—chicken strips tossed with egg noodles and crunchy vegetables for texture, flavor, color, and nutrients. This is not a saucy dish—everything is evenly coated with seasonings, and every mouthful is light but flavorful.

Ingredients

10 ounces medium egg noodles
3–4 tablespoons oil
1 onion, sliced
1.3 pounds chicken breast, cut into ½-inch strips
1 jalapeño, finely chopped
1 ounce fresh ginger, peeled and grated
3 garlic cloves, finely chopped
3 ounces cabbage, shredded
1 carrot, julienned
2 teaspoons five spice powder
1 teaspoon ground black pepper
1 teaspoon chili powder
5 tablespoons dark soy sauce
1 teaspoon white or rice vinegar
½ red pepper, thinly sliced
½ green pepper, thinly sliced
6–7 tablespoons chili crisp
2 tablespoons sriracha sauce
salt

GARNISH

2 spring onions, finely chopped
1 teaspoon nigella seeds
1 teaspoon toasted sesame seeds

Method

Cook the noodles according to the package instructions, drain, and set aside.

Heat the oil in a wok or large frying pan over medium heat and stir-fry the onion until soft and translucent. Add the chicken, jalapeño, ginger, and garlic and cook for about 25 minutes until the chicken is cooked through and there's only a little moisture left. Add the cabbage and carrot and stir for 3 minutes until the cabbage has almost wilted but still has a bite to it.

Add the five spice powder, black pepper, chili powder, soy sauce, vinegar, and red and green peppers, then season with salt. Add the chili crisp and sriracha for extra kick and stir-fry for another 2–3 minutes.

Add the noodles and toss everything together to coat them in the sauce. Serve garnished with spring onions, nigella seeds, and sesame seeds.

 TIP Feel free to adjust the spices and sauces if you like. Add more sauces if you like a wetter dish or more chili powder or sriracha if you like it spicy. Sliced beef or raw king prawns also make a great chow mein instead of the chicken.

Sticky Lamb Chops

MAKES
10

TIME
Prep: 20 minutes
Marinating: 1–2 hrs
Cook: 25–30 mins

My kids say these are the best lamb chops they have ever tasted. Sticky, saucy, and barbecue-y—I think you'll love them too!

Ingredients

10 lamb chops
1 teaspoon chili powder
1 teaspoon paprika
1 teaspoon garlic paste
1 teaspoon ground black pepper
1 tablespoon oil
chopped spring onion, to garnish

BARBECUE SAUCE
6 tablespoons tomato passata
2 tablespoons barbecue sauce
3 tablespoons honey
1 tablespoon Worcestershire sauce
1 teaspoon ground black pepper

Method

Place the lamb chops in a bowl, add the chili powder, paprika, garlic paste, and black pepper and mix to coat. Marinate in the fridge for 1–2 hours.

Heat the oil in a saucepan over medium heat, add the chops, and cook for 25 minutes, turning regularly, or until cooked to your liking. Remove from the pan and set aside.

Place all the sauce ingredients in the lamb pan and simmer for 2 minutes, then add the chops to the sauce and coat well. Serve garnished with chopped spring onion.

Egg-Fried Rice

This Indo-Chinese rice is loaded with veggies and fluffy scrambled eggs. Perfect on its own or as a side with Orange Chili Chicken (page 95) or Sweet & Sour Prawns (page 77).

Ingredients

1 cup water
4 ounces basmati rice
2 tablespoons butter
2 eggs
2 tablespoons oil
1 onion, diced
1 teaspoon ginger paste
1 teaspoon garlic paste
1 teaspoon chili paste
1 ounce carrot, grated
1 ounce cabbage, finely shredded
½ red pepper, diced
½ green pepper, diced
1 ounce canned corn, drained
1 ounce green beans
3 tablespoons chili sauce
1 tablespoon dark soy sauce
2 spring onions, finely chopped, plus extra
   to garnish
salt and ground black pepper

Method

Pour the water into a medium saucepan, bring to a boil, and add salt to taste. Add the rice and cook uncovered for 10–12 minutes until it is 80% cooked. It needs to be cooked on the outside, but the inside should be a little firm, as the rice will cook further when you fry it. Drain in a colander and set aside.

Heat the butter in a medium frying pan over medium heat, crack the eggs into the pan, and season with black pepper and salt. Scramble the eggs until cooked through, then remove from the pan and set aside.

Heat the oil in same pan, add the onion, ginger paste, garlic paste, chili paste, grated carrot, cabbage, red and green peppers, corn, and green beans. Stir-fry for a few minutes to soften the veggies, then add the chili sauce, soy sauce, and spring onions and season with salt.

Throw in the scrambled eggs, stir in, then add the rice and very gently stir, making sure not to break the rice. Cover the pan with a lid and cook over low heat for 10 minutes until the rice fluffs up and is cooked through. Serve garnished with spring onions.

Spicy Beef

SERVES 4

TIME
Prep: 20 minutes
Marinating: 30 mins
Cook: 10 minutes

This popular Chinese take-out dish is easy to re-create at home. Crispy fried beef is tossed in a spicy chili sauce—it's amazingly delicious and flavorful. What's not to love? Serve on a bed of noodles or Egg-Fried Rice (page 81).

Ingredients

1.1 pounds lean beef steak, cut into ¼-inch strips
1 tablespoon dark soy sauce
1 egg, beaten
1 tablespoon five spice powder
1 tablespoon ground black pepper
1 tablespoon rice vinegar
1 teaspoon ginger paste
1 teaspoon garlic paste
1 tablespoon sesame oil
2 tablespoons cornstarch
oil, for deep-frying

SPICY SAUCE

1 tablespoon sesame oil
1 red onion, thickly sliced
½ red pepper, thickly sliced
½ green pepper, thickly sliced
1 jalapeño, finely sliced
1 tablespoon dark soy sauce
1 tablespoon Worcestershire sauce
2 tablespoons chili crisp
1 teaspoon chili powder
1 tablespoon chili flakes
1 tablespoon ground black pepper
1 teaspoon salt

GARNISH

2 spring onions, julienned
1 teaspoon toasted sesame seeds

Method

Place the beef strips in a bowl with the soy sauce, beaten egg, five spice powder, black pepper, vinegar, ginger paste, garlic paste, and sesame oil. Mix well and leave to marinate for 30 minutes.

Place the cornstarch in a shallow bowl, add the beef, and toss to coat in the cornstarch.

Heat the oil for deep-frying in a large saucepan over medium-high heat until it reaches 350°F. Fry the beef strips in batches for 3 minutes until crispy and golden brown, then drain on paper towels.

For the spicy sauce, heat the sesame oil in a wok over medium-high heat, add all the remaining sauce ingredients, stir well, and cook for 3–4 minutes to soften the vegetables a little. Add the beef and stir to coat in the sauce. Serve garnished with spring onions and sesame seeds.

 If you want to include more veggies, you can also add baby corn and broccoli florets to this dish at the same times as the peppers.

Saucy Gazebo Chicken

SERVES
3–4

TIME
Prep: 20 minutes
Marinating: 1 hour
Cook: 30 minutes

Gazebo chicken is absolutely full of flavor—tasty, spicy, saucy, tender, and finger-licking good. Serve with rice or chips and salad.

Ingredients

1 chicken, cut into 8 pieces
1 tablespoon lemon juice
1 teaspoon salt
1 tablespoon ground black pepper
1 tablespoon white vinegar
3 tablespoons cornstarch
1 tablespoon atta flour
1–2 eggs, beaten
oil, for deep-frying

SAUCE
2 tablespoons oil
1 teaspoon garlic paste
½ teaspoon salt
1 teaspoon ground black pepper
1 teaspoon chili flakes
1 tablespoon chili powder
3 tablespoons ketchup
½ red pepper, cut into chunks
½ green pepper, cut into chunks

GARNISH
2 spring onions, finely chopped
0.5 ounce fresh cilantro, finely chopped

Method

Place the chicken pieces in a large bowl, add the lemon juice, salt, black pepper, and vinegar and leave to marinate in the fridge for 1 hour or overnight if possible.

For the sauce, heat the oil in a saucepan over low heat and add the garlic paste, salt, black pepper, chili flakes, chili powder, and ketchup. Cook over low heat for 2 minutes, then add the red and green peppers and cook for a further 3–4 minutes until softened but still with a little bite.

Take the chicken out of the fridge and add the cornstarch, atta, and enough beaten egg to coat the chicken all over. Mix well.

Heat the oil for deep-frying in a large saucepan over medium-high heat until it reaches 350°F. Fry the pieces of chicken for 10–12 minutes until cooked through, then drain on paper towels. Coat the chicken pieces in the sauce and garnish with spring onions and chopped cilantro.

Paneer & Cassava Sizzler

This is one of my favorite vegetarian dishes, something my mum makes when we have a get-together. The pieces of fried cheese and cassava are tossed into a spicy and tangy sauce. You really don't need anything else with it, it tastes so good just on its own.

Ingredients

7 ounces frozen cassava
3 tablespoons all-purpose flour
3 tablespoons cornstarch
1 tablespoon ground black pepper
1 teaspoon salt
½ cup water
7 ounces paneer, cut into 1-inch cubes
oil, for deep-frying
2 spring onions, finely chopped, to garnish

TANGY SAUCE
1 tablespoon oil
2 garlic cloves, chopped
2 tablespoons chili flakes
½ red pepper, cut into 1-inch chunks
½ green pepper, cut into 1-inch chunks
1 large onion, cut into 1-inch chunks
2 tablespoons ketchup
2 tablespoons sweet chili sauce
2 tablespoons dark soy sauce
3 tablespoons tamarind sauce, plus extra
    for drizzling
1 fresh tomato, chopped

TIP You can swap the paneer for firm tofu if you prefer.

Method

Place the cassava in a steamer and cook for 25 minutes, or until just tender with a slight bite to it. Do not overcook or it will become mushy. Alternatively, cook it in a saucepan of boiling water if you prefer. Cut the cassava into 1-inch chunks and set aside.

Place the all-purpose flour in a large bowl with the cornstarch, black pepper, and salt. Mix well, adding enough of the water to make a smooth, free-flowing batter. It should be neither thick nor thin. Set aside.

Heat the oil for deep-frying in a large saucepan over medium-high heat to 350°F. Fry the chunks of cassava in batches for 3–4 minutes until golden brown all over, then drain in a colander to remove excess oil.

Dip the paneer cubes in the batter and drop them carefully in batches into the hot oil. Fry until the paneer pieces are golden brown and crispy all over, then drain in the colander.

For the sauce, heat the oil in a large wok over medium-high heat. Add the garlic, chili flakes, red and green peppers, and onion and stir-fry for 3–4 minutes until the vegetables are softened but still have a bite to them. Add the ketchup, sweet chili sauce, soy sauce, tamarind sauce, and fresh tomato and cook for 3–4 minutes until the sauce thickens slightly.

Add the cassava chunks and paneer and toss to combine with the sauce. Garnish with spring onions and drizzle some extra tamarind sauce on top if you like it extra tangy.

Sweet & Sour Chicken

SERVES
4

TIME
Prep: 20 minutes
Marinating: 1–2 hrs
Cook: 10 minutes

This tantalizing, saucy, Indo-Chinese fried chicken really brings the sauces and spices together so well. This is a great combo of sweet and savory, and it tastes as good as it looks. It's a family favorite for us and might soon be for you too! Serve with fries and salad.

Ingredients

1.1 pounds chicken breast, cut into ½-inch strips
1 egg, beaten
1½ tablespoons dark soy sauce
1 teaspoon ginger paste
1 teaspoon garlic paste
1 teaspoon chili flakes
1 teaspoon ground cumin
1 teaspoon ground coriander
1 teaspoon ground black pepper
2 tablespoons cornstarch
2 tablespoons rice flour
2 tablespoons paprika
oil, for deep-frying

SWEET & SOUR SAUCE
2 tablespoons sesame oil
5–6 curry leaves
1 teaspoon chili paste
1 teaspoon sesame seeds
1 tablespoon dark soy sauce
1 teaspoon rice vinegar
9 ounces sweet chili sauce
2 tablespoons honey
3 tablespoons ketchup
½ red pepper, cut into ¼-inch slices
½ green pepper, cut into ¼-inch slices

GARNISH
finely chopped spring onions
1 teaspoon toasted sesame seeds

Method

Place the chicken in a bowl with the beaten egg, soy sauce, ginger paste, garlic paste, chili flakes, cumin, ground coriander, black pepper, cornstarch, rice flour, and paprika and marinate in the fridge for 1–2 hours.

For the sauce, heat a large wok over medium heat. Add the oil, curry leaves, chili paste, and sesame seeds and sizzle for 30–40 seconds—the curry leaves will give off a nutty, lemony aroma. Add the soy sauce, rice vinegar, sweet chili sauce, honey, ketchup, and the red and green peppers. Simmer the sauce over low heat for 5 minutes, then remove from the heat and set aside.

Heat the oil for deep-frying in a large saucepan over medium-high heat until it reaches 350°F. Fry the chicken strips in batches for 4–5 minutes, or until crispy and cooked through, taking care not to overcrowd the pan. Drain in a colander to remove excess oil.

Toss the fried chicken in the sauce, making sure to coat the chicken strips completely. Serve garnished with chopped spring onions and a sprinkling of sesame seeds.

Vegetable Noodles

SERVES

2

TIME

Prep: 20 minutes
Cook: 12 minutes

This is probably one of the easiest and most delicious noodle dishes to make. These noodles can be rustled up in no time at all. Perfect on their own or on the side with Sweet & Sour Chicken (page 88).

Ingredients

5 ounces medium egg noodles
2 tablespoons oil
2 garlic cloves, chopped
1 jalapeño, finely sliced
1 onion, finely sliced
2 ounces cabbage, finely shredded
2 ounces carrot, julienned
2 ounces green beans
½ red pepper, finely sliced
½ green pepper, finely sliced
2 tablespoons dark soy sauce
2 tablespoons chili sauce
1 teaspoon rice vinegar
1 teaspoon ground black pepper
1 teaspoon chili flakes
1 teaspoon salt

GARNISH
1 teaspoon toasted sesame seeds
finely chopped spring onions

Method

Cook the noodles according to the package instructions, drain, and set aside.

Heat the oil in a large wok over high heat. Add the garlic, sliced jalapeño, and onion and stir-fry for 2 minutes. Add the cabbage, carrot, green beans, and red and green peppers. Stir-fry for 3–4 minutes until softened but still with some bite. Do not overcook the veggies.

Reduce the heat to medium. Add the soy sauce, chili sauce, rice vinegar, black pepper, chili flakes, and salt and toss with the noodles for 2 minutes. Sprinkle with sesame seeds and chopped spring onions to garnish.

 TIP You could add snow peas, sugar snaps, frozen peas, or baby corn with the other vegetables if you fancy a change.

Lamb Stir-Fry

SERVES
2–3

TIME
Prep: 15 minutes
Cook: 20 minutes

This is a one-pot recipe—lamb, veggies, and noodles tossed together in a tangy, spicy sauce. It's so delicious, vibrant, and easy to make.

Ingredients

7 ounces medium egg noodles
5 ounces lean lamb steaks
2–3 garlic cloves, chopped
½ teaspoon chili flakes
1 teaspoon five spice powder
1 tablespoon honey
3 tablespoons Worcestershire sauce
1 tablespoon sriracha sauce
2 tablespoons sesame oil
1 fresh chili, finely chopped
1 ounce fresh ginger, peeled and chopped
5 ounces mixed stir-fry vegetables
1 tablespoon dark soy sauce

GARNISH
finely chopped fresh cilantro
finely chopped spring onions
½ teaspoon toasted sesame seeds
½ teaspoon nigella seeds

Method

Cook the noodles according to the package instructions, drain, and set aside.

Remove any fat from the lamb steaks and slice the meat into ½-inch strips. Place in a bowl with the garlic, chili flakes, five spice powder, honey, Worcestershire sauce, and sriracha sauce for that extra kick. Stir everything together and marinate for 10 minutes.

Heat the sesame oil in a wok over high heat, add the fresh chili and lamb strips (reserving the marinade), and stir-fry for 3–4 minutes to brown the meat. Add the chopped ginger, then pour in the reserved marinade, the stir-fry vegetables, noodles, and soy sauce. Toss everything together and cook for 2–3 minutes, until the vegetables are just tender.

Garnish with chopped cilantro and spring onions and sprinkle with sesame and nigella seeds to pretty it up. All done and you're ready to dive in!

Cauliflower Manchurian

SERVES
2–3

TIME
Prep: 15 minutes
Cook: 20 minutes

Also known as Gobi Manchurian, this popular Indo-Chinese dish has crispy cauliflower florets tossed in a spicy sauce.

Ingredients

1 cauliflower, cut into florets
1 tablespoon oil, plus extra for deep-frying
2 garlic cloves, chopped
1 fresh green chili, chopped
1 red onion, diced
2 spring onions, finely sliced, plus extra to garnish
½ red pepper, diced
½ green pepper, diced
2 tablespoons ketchup
2 tablespoons chili sauce
2 tablespoons dark soy sauce
1 tablespoon rice vinegar
1 tablespoon chili flakes
1 tablespoon ground black pepper
1 teaspoon salt

BATTER
¾ cup all-purpose flour
2 tablespoons cornstarch
1 teaspoon chili powder
1 teaspoon Kashmiri chili powder
1 teaspoon ground black pepper
1 teaspoon salt
1 cup water

Method

Cook the cauliflower florets in a large saucepan of boiling water for 8–10 minutes, then drain in a colander and set aside.

For the batter, mix all the dry ingredients together in a large bowl, then slowly add the water, stirring all the time to make a smooth batter thick enough to coat the cauliflower. Drop the florets into the batter and stir gently to coat.

Heat the oil for deep-frying in a large saucepan over medium-high heat until it reaches 350°F. Fry the cauliflower florets in batches for about 6 minutes until golden brown and crisp, then drain in a colander to remove excess oil.

Heat the oil in a large wok over low heat. Add the garlic, chopped chili, red onion, spring onions, and red and green peppers and cook, stirring, for 2 minutes. Add the ketchup, chili sauce, soy sauce, rice vinegar, chili flakes, black pepper, and salt and heat through for 1 minute.

Toss the fried florets in the sauce, making sure to coat them properly. Serve the cauliflower in a bowl, garnished with sliced spring onions.

Orange Chili Chicken

SERVES 5

TIME
Prep: 30 minutes
Marinating: 30 mins
Cook: 25 minutes

This Chinese-style chicken is definitely a popular dish in our home. Chunks of boneless chicken are fried until golden brown and crispy, then tossed in a sweet and spicy orange sauce, which is full of flavor. Serve with Vegetable Noodles (page 89) or Egg-Fried Rice (page 81).

Ingredients

1.3 pounds boneless chicken thighs or breast, cut into 1-inch pieces
2 tablespoons dark soy sauce
1 teaspoon white pepper
2 teaspoons five spice powder
1 tablespoon garlic, finely chopped
1 teaspoon salt
1 teaspoon baking soda
2 eggs, beaten
1 cup cornstarch
¼ cup water
oil, for deep-frying

ORANGE SAUCE
3 tablespoons dark soy sauce
2 teaspoons finely grated orange zest
6 tablespoons freshly squeezed orange juice
3 tablespoons brown sugar
2 tablespoons cornstarch
½ cup water
2 tablespoons oil
2 garlic cloves, finely chopped
1 tablespoon chili flakes
1 jalapeño, finely chopped
3 tablespoons chili sauce

GARNISH
1 teaspoon toasted sesame seeds
finely chopped spring onion
orange slices

Method

Place the chicken in a large bowl with the soy sauce, white pepper, five spice powder, garlic, salt, and baking soda and leave to marinate in the fridge for 30 minutes.

Whisk the eggs, cornstarch, and water together in another large bowl, add the marinated chicken, and toss to coat in the mixture.

Heat the oil for deep-frying in a large saucepan over medium-high heat until it reaches 350°F. Fry the chicken pieces in batches for 10 minutes, or until golden brown all over and cooked through, then drain on paper towels.

For the orange sauce, mix the soy sauce, orange zest and juice, sugar, cornstarch, and water together in a bowl and set aside.

Heat the oil in a large wok over low heat. Add the garlic, chili flakes, and jalapeño and cook for about 1 minute. Pour in the orange sauce and stir. Add the chili sauce and simmer gently for 8–10 minutes until it thickens slightly. Add the crispy fried chicken pieces and toss around until coated nicely. Sprinkle with sesame seeds and spring onions and garnish with orange slices.

PERFECT FOR A

Feast

A wonderful array of delights and a feast for all the senses, these dishes will create aromas to entice your family and friends into your kitchen to enjoy the deliciousness that awaits them. These are recipes that will welcome guests to the table from the moment they set their eyes on the platters.

Chicken Balti

SERVES

4

TIME

Prep: 25 minutes
Cook: 1 hour

After I got married, my mother-in-law made this delicious Chicken Balti for me—tender pieces of boneless chicken in an aromatic Balti curry sauce. The flavor is phenomenal with golden brown onions, tangy tomatoes, warm spices, a subtle taste of fenugreek, and the heat of the chilies—you will not be disappointed. Traditionally, a balti curry is served in or cooked in a metal bowl-like cooking vessel similar to a wok. Serve with Naan (pages 130–1), Roti (pages 126–7), or Basmati Rice (page 132).

Ingredients

9 ounces canned chopped tomatoes
6 tablespoons oil
2 onions, finely chopped
1.3 pounds chicken breast, cut into 1-inch chunks
1 teaspoon garlic paste
1 teaspoon ginger paste
1 tablespoon chili powder
1 tablespoon Kashmiri chili powder
1 teaspoon ground turmeric
1 tablespoon ground coriander
1 tablespoon ground cumin
½ teaspoon garam masala
1 teaspoon salt
1 tablespoon dried fenugreek leaves
1 fresh tomato, finely chopped
1 cup water
½ red pepper, cut into 1-inch chunks
½ green pepper, cut into 1-inch chunks
1 red onion, cut into chunks
finely chopped fresh cilantro, to garnish

WHOLE SPICES
1 teaspoon cumin seeds
2 bay leaves
2 cinnamon sticks
2–3 cardamom pods
5–6 black peppercorns
2–3 star anise
5–6 cloves

Method

Blitz the canned tomatoes in a food processor until smooth, then set aside.

Heat a large saucepan over medium heat. Add the oil, whole spices, and the onions and cook until the onions are nice and golden brown, stirring occasionally so they don't burn. Add the chicken, garlic paste, and ginger paste, stir, and cook for 25 minutes—the liquid released from the chicken will evaporate and you will see the oil coming through.

At this point, add the chili powder, Kashmiri chili powder, turmeric, ground coriander, cumin, garam masala, salt, and fenugreek. Cook the spices for 2 minutes, then add the puréed tomatoes and fresh tomato, stir, cover, and cook for 10–12 minutes over medium-low heat until the tomatoes have softened and dissolved. You should be able to smell the delicious aroma about now.

Pour in the water, add the red and green peppers and onion, and simmer over low heat for 8–10 minutes until the sauce thickens into a gravy-like consistency. Serve garnished with chopped cilantro.

TIP Adjust the amount of chili used in this recipe to your desired heat level. Adding whole spices makes the Chicken Balti so fragrant.

Naan Gosht

SERVES
6

TIME
Prep: 25 minutes
Cook: 1 hr 30 mins

My dear aunt Khadija probably makes the best version of this lamb curry I've ever tasted, and luckily she showed me how. The succulent lamb bathes in a thick rich gravy—that's what we love about this special and tantalizing dish. So aromatic, every mouthful is so full of flavor—from the caramelized onions and warm spices to the tangy tomatoes—one serving will not be enough. Traditionally, it's served with a type of fluffy bread (naan) to mop up the rich, spicy sauce; *gosht* means "meat," hence the name. It's a nostalgic dish for me, traditionally made on special occasions, so it holds amazing memories of my childhood. Serve with Basmati Rice (page 132), Naan (pages 130–1), and Classic Kachumbar Salad (page 122).

Ingredients

9 ounces canned chopped tomatoes
5 tablespoons oil
3 onions, finely chopped
1 heaping tablespoon ginger paste
1 heaping tablespoon garlic paste
2.2 pounds diced mixed lamb shoulder and leg
2 teaspoons ground black pepper
1 teaspoon ground turmeric
1 tablespoon ground coriander
1 tablespoon ground cumin
2 teaspoons chili powder
2 teaspoons Kashmiri chili powder
1 teaspoon tandoori masala
2 fresh tomatoes, finely diced
2 tablespoons tomato purée
about 2 cups water
salt

WHOLE SPICES
2 cinnamon sticks
2 bay leaves
4–5 black peppercorns
4–5 cardamom pods
4–5 cloves
1 teaspoon cumin seeds

GARNISH
chopped fresh cilantro
2–3 bullet chilies, sliced

Method

Blitz the canned tomatoes in a food processor until smooth, then set aside.

Heat the oil in a large saucepan over medium heat, add the whole spices, and fry for about 20 seconds until they start to sizzle. Add the onions and fry gently until they are meltingly soft, deeply browned, and rich. Do not rush this part—this step is important, as the overall color of the curry depends on it and it's one of the key steps in making an amazing curry.

Add the ginger paste and garlic paste and cook for 30 seconds to cook off the raw smell. Add the lamb, black pepper, and turmeric, stir, cover, and cook over medium heat for 30 minutes until the liquid from the meat has evaporated and the oil comes through to the top and sides of the pan.

Add the ground coriander, ground cumin, chili powder, Kashmiri chili powder, tandoori masala, fresh tomatoes, puréed tomatoes, and tomato purée and cook until the tomatoes soften and dissolve. Season with salt and pour in some water, depending on how thick or thin you want the curry. I prefer a gravy-like consistency. Simmer until the curry thickens and the meat is tender, then garnish with chopped cilantro and sliced bullet chilies.

 Peel and halve 5–6 baby potatoes, deep-fry until cooked and golden brown, then pop them in your curry just before serving.

Veggie Biryani

SERVES
3–4

TIME
Prep: 30 minutes
Cook: 55 minutes

Biryani is a rice dish made with layers of rice, spices, and usually meat, but this recipe is for vegetable lovers. Packed with veggies, warm spices like garam masala, and fresh cilantro and mint, this is a perfect hearty meal, super-delicious and bursting with flavor. Serve with Sweet Yogurt Lassi (page 145) and Mint & Cilantro Yogurt Chutney (page 137).

Ingredients

2 tablespoons ghee
2 tablespoons store-bought fried onions
2 tablespoons finely chopped fresh cilantro
2 tablespoons finely chopped fresh mint
½ red pepper, cut into 1-inch chunks
½ green pepper, cut into 1-inch chunks
⅓ cup water
1 lemon, cut into wedges, to serve

RICE
1.3 pounds basmati rice
6½ cups water
2 tablespoons oil
1 tablespoon salt

VEGETABLE MASALA
4 tablespoons oil
2 onions, finely diced
1 teaspoon ginger paste
1 teaspoon garlic paste
2 teaspoons chili paste
9 ounces frozen mixed vegetables
1 potato, cut into quarters
1 small eggplant, cut into 1-inch chunks
1 serving Vegetable Biryani Masala (page 169)
½ red pepper, cut into 1-inch chunks
½ green pepper, cut into 1-inch chunks
2 tablespoons finely chopped fresh cilantro

3 tablespoons finely chopped fresh mint
2 tablespoons chopped spring onion
4 ounces plain yogurt

WHOLE SPICES
1–2 cinnamon sticks
3–4 cloves
3–4 black peppercorns
2–3 cardamom pods
1–2 bay leaves
1–2 star anise
1 teaspoon cumin seeds

Method

Wash the rice in a sieve under cold running water until the water runs clear, then soak in a bowl of cold water for 30 minutes. This will reduce the cooking time and help the rice to cook evenly.

Pour the water into a large saucepan, bring to a boil, and add the oil and salt. Add the rice and cook uncovered for 8–10 minutes until it is 70%–75% cooked. It needs to be cooked on the outside but the inside should be a little firm, as the rice will cook further when you cook the biryani. Drain in a colander, then rinse under cold running water to stop it from cooking further. Drain very well, spread the rice on a large plate, and leave to cool completely, so the grains are separate and the rice does not go mushy.

For the vegetable masala, heat the oil in a large saucepan over low heat, then add the whole spices. Stir and let the spices sizzle for a few seconds. Add the onions and fry for 15 minutes until golden brown.

Add the ginger paste, garlic paste, and chili paste and cook for 2 minutes until the raw smell goes away.

Add the frozen mixed vegetables, potato, eggplant, and the Vegetable Biryani Masala spices. Cover and cook over medium heat for about 15 minutes until the potato is almost cooked. (If the pan is looking too dry and not enough steam is building from the frozen veggies, add some water to help the potato cook.) Add the red and green peppers, fresh cilantro, mint, and spring onion, and it's already smelling so good. Stir in the yogurt to give a creamy consistency.

Grease the bottom of a wide saucepan with ghee and arrange half the rice in an even layer in the bottom. Top with the vegetable masala, then the remaining rice on top in an even layer. Scatter with the fried onions, chopped cilantro and mint, and red and green pepper chunks.

Poke some holes in the rice to allow steam to escape and drizzle the water into the holes. Dot the remaining ghee on top of the rice to add extra flavor. Cover the saucepan with a tight-fitting lid so the steam doesn't escape and cook over low heat for 15 minutes. With the buildup of steam, the rice will finish cooking and fluff up, and the biryani will be ready. Serve with lemon wedges for squeezing.

 Long-grain basmati rice is best for making a good biryani.

 If you have time, crush your own fresh ginger, garlic, and chilies into a paste using a pestle and mortar. It makes all the difference.

Beef Kheema Pilau

SERVES
2–3

TIME
Prep: 40 minutes
Cook: 55 minutes

Being a busy mum, I know how difficult life can get. If you are looking for a hearty, soulful, gloriously aromatic meal but are short on time, this one-pot dish is perfect for you, especially during Ramadan, when you have so many things going on. Rice is a staple in our home—it's tasty, filling, and best of all, really easy to make. Spices are key for any pilau, and here the fragrant smell and taste come from the whole spices, cumin, cilantro, and garam masala. This pilau is perfect when you have guests round—as soon as they enter your home, the aroma will most definitely be inviting. Serve with Sweet Yogurt Lassi (page 145) and Classic Kachumbar Salad (page 122).

Ingredients

11 ounces basmati rice
3 tablespoons oil
1 onion, finely chopped
1 teaspoon chili paste
1 teaspoon ginger paste
1 teaspoon garlic paste
1.1 pounds ground beef
1 teaspoon ground cumin
1 teaspoon ground coriander
1 teaspoon chili powder
1 teaspoon ground black pepper
1 teaspoon garam masala
4¼ cups water
salt

WHOLE SPICES

½ teaspoon cumin seeds
1–2 cinnamon sticks
1–2 bay leaves
3–4 cardamom pods
3–4 black peppercorns
3–4 cloves
1–2 star anise

GARNISH

finely chopped fresh cilantro
lemon wedges

Method

Wash the rice in a sieve under cold running water until the water runs clear, then soak in a bowl of cold water for 30 minutes. This will reduce the cooking time and help the rice to cook evenly.

Heat the oil in a large saucepan over medium heat, add the whole spices, and fry for about 30–40 seconds until they start to sizzle. Add the onion and fry gently until it is meltingly soft, deeply browned, and rich. Do not rush this part—this step is important, as the color of the onion will determine the color of the finished dish. If not browned enough, the rice will look pale—we want to achieve a beige-brown color.

Add 3–4 tablespoons of water and simmer for 1–2 minutes to soften the onion and release a lovely brownish tinge. Add the chili paste, ginger paste, and garlic paste and cook over low heat for about 1 minute to cook off the raw smell.

Add the ground beef and stir, making sure to break up the lumps. The color will turn from pink to brown and the beef will start to release liquid. Cook over medium heat for 20 minutes until only a little moisture is left. At this point, add the cumin, ground coriander, chili powder, black pepper, and garam masala to give the dish some warming flavor and aroma. Cook for 1–2 minutes, stirring so the spices are mixed in nicely.

Add the rice to the pot and mix in with the kheema, then pour in the water, season with salt, and stir. Partially cover the pan with a lid (not completely or the water may boil over). Cook over medium heat for 15 minutes until the water has been absorbed, then give it a stir once without disturbing the rice too much. Cover fully with the lid and cook for another 15 minutes over low heat—with the buildup of steam, the rice will fully cook and fluff up. Serve on a large platter, garnished with chopped cilantro and lemon wedges.

 If you like, you can add some garden peas to this pilau to add a pop of color, sweetness, and texture. Throw them in when you add the rice.

Peri-Peri Sea Bass

SERVES
2–3

TIME
Prep: 25 minutes
Marinating: 30 mins
Cook: 30 minutes

Sea bass is a delicate white fish with soft flaky flesh. Here it's prepared in a tangy peri-peri marinade with fresh cilantro and chili to add a little kick. You could also use red snapper, sea bream, or gray mullet if you prefer. Serve with Basmati Rice (page 132) and lettuce leaves.

Ingredients

2 whole sea bass (12 ounces each), gutted and scaled
½ teaspoon sea salt
1 teaspoon ground black pepper
2 lemons
5 tablespoons olive oil
2 tablespoons peri-peri seasoning
1 tablespoon paprika
1 tablespoon garlic paste
1 fresh chili
1 ounce fresh cilantro, chopped, plus extra to garnish
1 lime, cut into wedges, to serve

Method

Wash the sea bass inside and out and pat dry with paper towels. Use a sharp knife to make 3–4 deep slashes on both sides of each fish to help the flesh cook evenly. Season the sea bass with the sea salt and freshly ground black pepper.

Juice one of the lemons and slice the other. Place the olive oil in a shallow dish with the peri-peri seasoning, paprika, garlic paste, and lemon juice. Blitz the fresh chili and cilantro to a paste in a food processor and mix in. Lay the fish in the dish and coat inside and out in the marinade, rubbing it into the slashes. Lay the lemon slices on top and marinate in the fridge for 30 minutes.

Preheat the oven to 350°F and line a roasting pan with foil. Lift the marinated fish into the pan and cook uncovered in the oven for about 25 minutes until the fish is cooked through—the flesh should feel firm to the touch and should be flaky and white. Garnish with chopped cilantro and serve with lime wedges.

 TIP Check that the fish is fresh before you buy—the eyes should be clear and slightly bulging, the gills should be a nice bright red, and the flesh should be firm and shiny.

Vegetable Karahi

Try this for a lighter iftar meal, packed with vegetables in a spicy masala made with warm spices, curry leaves to infuse some warmth, and chili powder to add heat. My grandmother used to make this delicious curry in a karahi, a deep wok traditionally made of cast iron, used in South Asian cooking. It distributes heat evenly, browns meats better, cooks vegetables faster, and lasts a lifetime. If you don't own one, you can still make this dish in a nonstick pot. Just as delish!

Ingredients

1 potato, peeled and cut into 1-inch chunks
1 carrot, peeled and cut into ½-inch slices
1 small dhoodi (bottle gourd), peeled and cut into 1-inch chunks
1 eggplant, cut into 1-inch chunks
1 drumstick (moringa), peeled and cut into finger-length pieces
2 onions
7 ounces canned chopped tomatoes
4 tablespoons oil
5–6 curry leaves
1 teaspoon ginger paste
1 teaspoon garlic paste
1 teaspoon chili paste
4 ounces frozen peas
4 ounces canned corn, drained
1 tablespoon ground cumin
1 tablespoon ground coriander
1 teaspoon chili powder
½ teaspoon ground turmeric
¼ cup water
½ red pepper, chopped into 1-inch chunks
½ green pepper, chopped into 1-inch chunks
salt
chopped fresh cilantro, to garnish

Method

Heat a large saucepan of boiling water over high heat. Add the potato, carrot, dhoodi, eggplant, and drumstick and cook for 15–20 minutes until the vegetables are almost tender but still have a bite. Drain in a colander and set aside.

Dice one onion finely and purée the other onion in a food processor to give the karahi texture. Remove from the food processor and blitz the tomatoes in it until smooth, then set aside.

Heat a large, wide saucepan over medium heat, then add the oil, curry leaves, and all the onions. Cover and cook for 15 minutes until golden brown. Add the ginger paste, garlic paste, and chili paste and cook for 1 minute to cook off the rawness. Add the partially cooked vegetables, peas, corn, ground cumin, ground coriander, chili powder, turmeric, and puréed tomatoes. Season with salt and mix gently, making sure not to break the vegetables.

Cover and cook over medium heat for 10–15 minutes. Add the water and red and green peppers and cook for a further 5–6 minutes. Serve garnished with chopped cilantro.

 You can also add sliced zucchini with the peppers—so healthy and delicious and no need to peel.

 To add some creamy goodness to your karahi, you could stir in 4–5 tablespoons of coconut milk.

King Prawn & Fish Curry

SERVES
4–5

TIME
Prep: 30 minutes
Marinating: 30 mins
Cook: 40 minutes

My grandmother regularly made this aromatic and colorful curry. I remember early morning visits to the fish shop to buy fresh fish and prawns—my grandmother would tell me what to look for when buying fresh seafood. This is a quick-and-easy recipe, made even easier if you ask your fishmonger to fillet the fish for you. Any white fish works well in this recipe—try cod, whiting, or mullet. Perfect with Khitchri (page 56–7) or Roti (pages 126–7).

Ingredients

4 tablespoons lemon juice
1 teaspoon chili paste
2 teaspoons garlic paste
1 teaspoon ground cumin
1 teaspoon ground coriander
½ teaspoon ground turmeric
1 tablespoon chopped fresh dill
10 ounces whitefish fillets, cut into 2-inch chunks
7 ounces raw king prawns, peeled and deveined
1 large fresh tomato
5 tablespoons oil
1 teaspoon cumin seeds
5–6 curry leaves
2 onions, finely diced
1 tablespoon tomato passata
½ cup water

GARNISH

0.5 ounce fresh cilantro, chopped
2 spring onions, finely chopped

Method

Place the lemon juice in a large bowl with the chili paste, garlic paste, ground cumin, ground coriander, turmeric, and dill. Add the fish and prawns and mix to coat all over. Marinate in the fridge for 30 minutes.

Use a knife to make a shallow X on the bottom of the tomato, then place in a bowl of boiling water for 40–50 seconds until the skin starts to peel off easily. Skin and finely chop the tomato and set aside.

Heat the oil in a large frying pan with a lid over medium heat, then add the cumin seeds and curry leaves—they will start to sizzle and smell fragrant. Stir in the onions and fry, uncovered, until lightly golden brown. Add the chopped tomato and passata and cook for 4–5 minutes until the tomato softens and dissolves.

Add the fish and prawns, cover, and cook over medium heat for 25 minutes, carefully turning the fish and prawns halfway without breaking the fish. Add the water and simmer for 6–8 minutes until slightly thickened. Serve garnished with chopped cilantro and spring onions.

 TIP Fresh fish shouldn't smell fishy or have a strong smell, just a clean, fresh smell of the sea. Press your finger against the body of the fish—it should be firm and spring back to the touch.

Beef Kofta Curry

Tender, juicy beef meatballs are simmered in a luscious, aromatic, and saucy curry, full of fragrant Indian spices. This is one of my husband's favorite curries and one he likes to make himself for the family. You could use ground chicken or lamb if you prefer. Serve with Roti (pages 126–7) or Naan (pages 130–1).

Ingredients

1.1 pounds ground beef
2 fresh chilies
0.2 ounce fresh cilantro
1 onion, quartered
1 teaspoon chili powder
1 tablespoon ground coriander
1 tablespoon ground cumin
1 teaspoon ground black pepper
½ teaspoon salt
1 teaspoon ginger paste
1 teaspoon garlic paste
5 ounces fresh bread crumbs

CURRY
5–6 tablespoons oil
2 onions, grated
1 teaspoon ginger paste
1 teaspoon garlic paste
14 ounces tomato passata
1 serving of Perfect Curry Spice Mix (page 169)
1⅔ cups water

WHOLE SPICES
2 cinnamon sticks
4–5 black peppercorns
4–5 cloves
3–4 cardamom pods
1 bay leaf
1 teaspoon cumin seeds
1–2 star anise

GARNISH
½ teaspoon garam masala
finely chopped fresh cilantro

Method

Place the ground beef in a food processor with the fresh chilies, fresh cilantro, and onion and blitz until the mixture is almost smooth but still has texture to it. This will help bind the ingredients together to form the meatballs. Add the chili powder, ground coriander, cumin, black pepper, salt, ginger paste, garlic paste, and bread crumbs and mix everything together.

Rub some oil on the palms of your hands and roll the beef mixture into smooth meatballs about 1 inch across. Place on a tray and set aside in the fridge while you prepare the curry.

For the curry, heat the oil in a large saucepan over medium heat, add the whole spices and sizzle for 30–40 seconds, then add the onions and fry until golden brown. Add the ginger paste and garlic paste and cook for 30–40 seconds to cook off the raw smell.

Arrange the meatballs in the pan, cover, and cook for 25 minutes, making sure to turn them gently halfway through so they don't stick to the pan. Once the liquid from the meatballs has evaporated and the oil comes through to the top, add the tomato passata and Perfect Curry Spice Mix. Stir the mixture carefully, making sure not to disturb the meatballs too much; otherwise, they can break.

Cover the pan and cook for 15 minutes until the passata starts to reduce. Pour in the water and simmer over low heat for 12–15 minutes until the curry starts to thicken. The aroma around your home will be just amazing. Serve garnished with garam masala to add some warmth and chopped cilantro to add some freshness.

 TIP You can make the meatballs in advance and freeze them raw on a tray, then pack them into plastic bags. They will keep for up to a month in the freezer and come in handy on those busy days.

Lamb Biryani

Biryani is a luxurious, elaborate, colorful, and highly aromatic dish, so it's traditionally made on special occasions. It's full of flavor, with spices and fresh herbs; perfectly cooked, fragrant, fluffy grains of basmati rice; and tender spiced lamb on the bone. When I was growing up, my grandmother would wake up early on Eid to make a big pot of Lamb Biryani, the main meal for the whole family to gather around. My mum would go early to give her a hand, and I would stand and watch and give the masala a taste test. The house would be so fragrant, you could smell the aroma outside. Serve with Sweet Yogurt Lassi (page 145), Mint & Cilantro Yogurt Chutney (page 137), and poppadoms.

Ingredients

1 teaspoon saffron threads
2 tablespoons milk
2 tablespoons ghee
0.5 ounce fresh cilantro leaves, finely chopped
0.5 ounce fresh mint leaves, finely chopped
2–3 green bullet chilies, halved
½ red pepper, cut into ½-inch dice
½ green pepper, cut into ½-inch dice
⅓ cup water
1 tablespoon pomegranate seeds, to garnish

RICE

1.5 pounds basmati rice
11 cups water
3 tablespoons oil
1 tablespoon salt
2 bay leaves
2 cinnamon sticks

LAMB MASALA

2.2 pounds mixed lamb shoulder and leg chunks
4 ounces plain yogurt
1 teaspoon chili paste
1 tablespoon ginger paste
1 tablespoon garlic paste
1 serving of Meat Biryani Masala (page 169)
2 tablespoons finely chopped fresh mint
2 tablespoons finely chopped fresh cilantro
5 tablespoons oil, plus extra for deep-frying
5 onions, finely sliced
3 tablespoons ghee
1 teaspoon salt
4 tablespoons lemon juice
1 cup water

WHOLE SPICES

1 teaspoon cumin seeds
2–3 cinnamon sticks
2–3 bay leaves
5–6 black peppercorns
5–6 cardamom pods
5–6 cloves
1–2 star anise

Method

The first step is to marinate the lamb. Place the lamb in a bowl with the yogurt (to tenderize it), the chili paste, ginger paste, and garlic paste, the Biryani Masala spices, and the fresh mint and cilantro. Cover and marinate in the fridge for about 1 hour to let the meat marinate.

Heat the oil for deep-frying in a large saucepan over medium-high heat until it reaches 350°F. Fry the sliced onions until

continued

nice and golden brown, making sure not to burn them. Drain on paper towels and set aside.

Wash the rice in a sieve under cold running water until the water runs clear, then soak in a bowl of cold water for 30 minutes. This will reduce the cooking time and help the rice to cook evenly.

Pour the water into a large pot, bring to a boil, and add the oil, salt, bay leaves, and cinnamon sticks. Add the rice and cook uncovered for 8–10 minutes until it is 70%–75% cooked. It needs to be cooked on the outside but the inside should be a little firm, as the rice will cook further when you cook the biryani. Drain in a colander, then rinse under cold running water to stop it from cooking further. Drain very well, spread the rice on a large plate, and leave to cool completely so the grains are separate and the rice does not go mushy.

For the lamb masala, heat the ghee in a large saucepan over low heat, add the whole spices, and allow to gently infuse in the oil for about 30 seconds. Add the marinated meat, stir, and turn the heat up to medium. Cover and cook for 30 minutes, stirring occasionally to make sure the meat doesn't stick or burn. If you have a pressure cooker, this will cut your cooking time in half. The lamb will release liquid as it cooks. Once the liquid has evaporated, sprinkle with the salt, then add the lemon juice, water, and half the fried onions, keeping the rest for garnish. Mix everything in and cook for 15 minutes over low heat until the

lamb is tender and the onions soften. The sauce will reduce and thicken.

Place the saffron threads in a small frying pan over very low heat and warm through, taking care as the strands burn easily. When slightly crisp, crush with the back of a spoon and add to the milk.

Grease the bottom of a wide saucepan with ghee and arrange half the rice in an even layer in the bottom. Top with the lamb masala and sprinkle with a few of the remaining fried onions, some of the chopped cilantro and mint, and the halved bullet chilies, then add the remaining rice on top in an even layer. Drizzle the saffron-infused milk on top to add aroma and color to the rice, then finally top with the red and green pepper chunks, the remaining chopped cilantro and mint, and the remaining fried onions.

Poke some holes in the rice to allow steam to escape and drizzle the water into the holes. Dot the remaining ghee on the top of the rice to add extra flavor. Cover the saucepan with a tight-fitting lid so the steam doesn't escape, and cook over low heat for 20 minutes. With the buildup of steam, the rice will finish cooking and fluff up, and the biryani will be ready. Serve on a large platter, garnished with pomegranate seeds to add a pop of color.

 You can also add a splash of rosewater on top of the rice when adding the saffron-infused milk to add extra aroma.

Chicken & Potato Curry

SERVES
3–4

TIME
Prep: 20 minutes
Cook: 1 hr 10 mins

Chicken & Potato Curry is one of the easiest curries you can make, and it's delicious too, which is why it's been ever so popular since I can remember. The traditional authentic spices make this curry spicy, fragrant, rich, and a staple in most Indian homes. Serve with Basmati Rice (page 132), Roti (pages 126–7), or Naan (pages 130–1).

Ingredients

4 tablespoons oil
2 onions, finely chopped
1 whole chicken, cut into 8 pieces
1 teaspoon ginger paste
1 teaspoon garlic paste
9 ounces canned chopped tomatoes
1 teaspoon chili powder
1 teaspoon ground cumin
1 teaspoon ground coriander
½ teaspoon ground turmeric
½ teaspoon ground black pepper
1 tablespoon tomato purée
2 potatoes, peeled and quartered
2 cups water
½ teaspoon salt

WHOLE SPICES
½ teaspoon cumin seeds
1–2 cinnamon sticks
3–4 cardamom pods
3–4 black peppercorns
3–4 cloves
1–2 star anise

GARNISH
½ teaspoon garam masala
chopped fresh cilantro

Method

Heat the oil in a large saucepan over medium heat, add the whole spices, and fry for about 20 seconds until they start to sizzle. Add the onions and fry gently until they are meltingly soft, deeply browned, and rich. Do not rush this part—this step is important, as the overall color of the curry depends on it and it's one of the key steps in making an amazing curry.

Add the chicken, ginger paste, and garlic paste, stir gently, and cover the pan with a lid. Cook for 20–30 minutes until the liquid that is released from the chicken evaporates.

Blitz the canned tomatoes in a food processor until smooth. Add to the pan with the chili powder, cumin, ground coriander, turmeric, black pepper, and tomato purée and stir in. Cover and cook for 20 minutes until the oil comes through to the top and sides of the pan.

Add the potatoes, water, and salt and simmer over low heat for another 20 minutes until the curry thickens slightly and the potatoes are tender but not too soft or they will break. Serve garnished with the garam masala and chopped cilantro to add some freshness to the curry.

Beef Bhuna

SERVES
6

TIME
Prep: 30 minutes
Marinating: 1 hour
Cook: 1 hour 30 mins
(If you have a pressure cooker, this will cut your cooking time in half)

This is the ultimate Beef Bhuna recipe, perfect for Ramadan—my dad's absolute favorite and now mine. My mum showed me how to make this and I want you to try it for your family. Bhuna means "to fry," and here the beef is fried in aromatic spices, such as mustard seeds, nigella seeds, and fenugreek, which intensify the flavor. The tomatoes and onions give a rich, thick base to the curry. This is so comforting, hearty, and packed full of flavor. Enjoy with Naan (pages 130–1), Roti (pages 126–7), or Basmati Rice (page 132).

Ingredients

2.2 pounds beef chunks, with or without bones
2 tablespoons ginger paste
2 tablespoons garlic paste
1 heaping tablespoon ground turmeric
2 ounces plain yogurt

MASALA
6 tablespoons oil
5–6 onions, finely sliced
1 serving of Bhuna Masala (page 169)
2 plum tomatoes
2 cups water

WHOLE SPICES
1 teaspoon cumin seeds
½ teaspoon mustard seeds
2 bay leaves
5–6 cloves
5–6 black peppercorns
3–4 cinnamon sticks
3–4 star anise

GARNISH
2 bullet chilies, sliced
finely chopped fresh cilantro

Method

Place the beef in a bowl with the ginger paste, garlic paste, turmeric, and yogurt, mix well, and leave to marinate in the fridge for 1 hour or overnight.

For the masala, heat the oil in a large saucepan over medium heat, add the whole spices, and fry for about 20 seconds until they start to sizzle. Add the onions and fry gently until they are meltingly soft, deeply browned, and rich. Do not rush this part—this step is important, as the overall color of the curry depends on it and it's one of the key steps in making an amazing curry.

Add the marinated meat, stir well, and cook for about 25 minutes over low heat—the meat will cook in its own juices. When only a little moisture is left, add the Bhuna Masala spices.

Use a knife to make a shallow X on the bottom of the tomatoes, then place in a bowl of boiling water for 40–50 seconds until the skin starts to peel off easily. Skin and finely chop the tomatoes, add to the saucepan, and cook for 15 minutes until the tomatoes soften and dissolve, adding texture to the sauce.

Add the water, stir well, cover, and cook gently for about 45 minutes, or until the water has evaporated and the oil comes through to the top, stirring occasionally.

When the meat is tender, remove the lid, turn up the heat, and fry the curry to reduce the sauce to a thick, gravy-like consistency. Serve garnished with sliced bullet chilies and chopped cilantro.

SALADS, BREADS &

Chutneys

Something on the side? These recipes are sure
to complement your mains nicely. I don't know
about you, but I always need something to
crunch on with my curry or dip my savory
snacks in—I've got you covered for whatever
delicious food is on your table!

Classic Kachumbar Salad

SERVES
4–5

TIME
Prep: 15 minutes

Kachumbar may look like a basic salad, but it is one of the most popular—so refreshing, it adds crunch, color, and texture and makes an appearance with so many dishes, including curries, rice, burgers, and tacos. Kachumbar will brighten up any meal.

Ingredients

2 tomatoes, finely diced
1 cucumber, finely diced
1 red onion, finely diced
2 tablespoons fresh cilantro, chopped
salt
ground black pepper
lemon juice, for squeezing

Method

Place the tomatoes, cucumber, red onion, and cilantro in a colander and leave to drain for 15 minutes to remove the excess liquid. Transfer to a bowl and season with salt, pepper, and a squeeze of lemon just before serving.

 TIP Stir a finely chopped fresh chili in to add some kick to your kachumbar.

Watermelon, Feta & Mint Salad

SERVES

2

TIME

Prep: 5 minutes

Absolutely delicious and refreshing, this summery salad combines sweet, juicy cubes of watermelon with salty, creamy feta and crisp, colorful red onions with a sprinkling of fresh, scented mint leaves. Serve alongside Masala Roast Chicken (page 72).

Ingredients

10 ounces watermelon, rind removed, cubed
1 ounce Kalamata olives
½ small red onion, finely sliced
2 ounces feta, cubed
1 tablespoon fresh mint leaves, finely chopped

Method

Place the watermelon, olives, and red onion in a large bowl and give them a gentle toss. Finish off with the feta and a sprinkling of chopped mint.

 TIP Choose a ripe watermelon, as the flavor will be better—look for a dark green, dull-looking melon. The heaviest melons are usually the ripest.

Chana Chaat

SERVES
2

TIME
**Prep and Cook:
25 minutes**

Chana Chaat is a tasty, quick, and easy-to-assemble vegetarian salad, a popular street food snack that is bursting with flavor. I have used basic spices, canned chickpeas to give a salty taste, potatoes to add some bite, fresh tomatoes to add sweetness, red onions to give it crunch, yogurt for a creamy texture, and tamarind sauce to give it some tang! All the flavors really complement each other so well. There are different variations of chaat but this one can be served alongside any rice dish, such as pilau or biryani.

Ingredients

10 ounces potatoes, peeled and cubed
2 x 14-ounce cans chickpeas, drained
1 large red onion, finely diced
2 fresh tomatoes, finely diced
10 ounces plain yogurt
2 fresh chilies, finely chopped
½ teaspoon chili powder
½ teaspoon mango powder or chaat masala
½ teaspoon salt

TO SERVE
3 tablespoons tamarind sauce
0.5 ounce fresh cilantro, finely chopped
2 tablespoons pomegranate seeds

Method

Cook the potato cubes in a saucepan of boiling water for 15–20 minutes, or until just tender. Drain and set aside to cool.

Place the potato in a large bowl with all the remaining ingredients and mix together well. Serve in bowls, drizzled with tamarind sauce and garnished with chopped cilantro and pomegranate seeds to add a pop of color.

Roti

Nothing beats the smell of fresh homemade roti—pillow-soft, fluffy, light, and airy flatbreads with charred spots adding a subtle flavor and texture. This is a staple in most Indian homes, served with curries to mop up the sauce. I remember standing by my mum's side, eagerly awaiting a fresh roti off the tawa (skillet). She would grab an open package of butter, fold the wrapping back, and spread the actual block as it melted and oozed all over the hot bread—then she'd add a good sprinkling of sugar before rolling it up, ready for me to enjoy. I always remember those good days! Now I do exactly the same with my children . . . and I make one for myself too.

Ingredients

2 cups atta flour or whole wheat flour, plus extra for rolling
2 tablespoons ghee or butter
1¾–2 cups boiling water
oil, for kneading

Method

Place the flour in a large bowl, add the ghee, and rub it into the flour with your fingertips for about 3 minutes until the mixture resembles bread crumbs. Make a well in the middle of the bowl and slowly pour in the boiling water bit by bit, just enough to form a soft dough. Mix with your hands for about a minute until there is no flour left at the bottom of the bowl. The dough shouldn't be too dry or too sticky.

Transfer the dough to a lightly floured surface and knead with your hands for 5–8 minutes until it becomes soft and pliable—the longer you knead it, the softer the rotis. You can put a little oil on your hands while kneading so it doesn't stick to your fingers. Divide the dough into 6 equal-sized balls, pop them back in the bowl, and cover with a damp cloth to prevent them from drying out.

Roll one of the balls in a little flour and flatten it a bit with your hands. Use a rolling pin to roll it out on a lightly floured surface into a 6- to 7-inch disk, about ¼ inch thick. Repeat with the other balls of dough.

Heat a tawa, nonstick frying pan, or griddle over high heat until hot. Place a roti on the pan and cook for 30 seconds, or until you see tiny dots appear on the surface. Flip over with a clean kitchen towel or your hand (carefully!) and cook on the other side for 30 seconds. Take a look underneath and, if you see golden-brown spots, flip the roti over again and gently press on top with a folded kitchen towel—the whole roti will start to puff up. Wrap the cooked rotis in a clean kitchen towel to keep them warm and soft while you cook the rest.

Leftover rotis can be wrapped in foil and stored in an airtight container for up to 2 days to keep them fresh. You can batch-cook rotis for future use—allow to cool fully, then place the rotis in a plastic bag with parchment paper between them and freeze flat in your freezer. When you need them, defrost for 20 minutes and heat one by one in a hot pan.

 You can also make roti dough in a stand mixer, using a dough hook.

Naan

These are the fluffiest and softest naan, perfect with any curry. Or you can eat them on their own—just brush with ghee or garlic butter . . . so buttery and tasty! These Indian-style flatbreads are traditionally made in a tandoor or clay oven, but you can bake them in a hot oven or cook on the stovetop and watch them puff up right in front of you. Serve warm with stews and curries, such as Butter Chicken (page 67) and Naan Gosht (pages 100–1) to mop up the sauce. Delicious!

Ingredients

1 teaspoon sugar
2¼ teaspoons dried yeast
½ cup warm water
3¾ cups bread flour, plus extra for dusting
4 ounces plain yogurt
½ teaspoon salt
1 tablespoon oil
3 tablespoons melted butter
1 teaspoon poppy seeds or sesame seeds

Method

To bloom the yeast, place the sugar, yeast, and warm water in a pitcher, cover with a damp cloth, and set aside for 10 minutes until it becomes foamy. This step will make the naan fluffier and softer.

Place the flour in a large bowl, make a well in the middle, and pour in the yogurt, salt, and oil. Slowly add the yeast mixture a little at a time, mixing as you go. Once the flour is mostly incorporated, use your hands to bring it together into a ball.

Transfer the dough to a lightly floured surface and knead with your hands for 10 minutes. Alternatively, knead it in a stand mixer with a dough hook. Pop the dough into a greased bowl, cover with a damp cloth, and leave to rise in a warm place for 1 hour, or until the dough doubles in size.

Preheat the oven to 500°F or as hot as it will go and line a baking sheet with parchment paper.

Once the dough has risen, knead again on a lightly floured surface for 1 minute, then divide the dough into 5 equal-sized balls. Roll one of the balls in a little flour and flatten it a bit with your hands. Use a rolling pin or your hands to shape it on a lightly floured surface into a 7- to 8-inch oval shape. Repeat with the other balls of dough. Place the naan on the prepared baking sheet, brush with the melted butter, and sprinkle with poppy or sesame seeds.

Cook in the oven for 3–4 minutes—they are ready when the naan start to puff up and turn golden brown and the undersides are slightly charred. You can also cook them on the hob. Heat a tawa, nonstick frying pan, or griddle over high heat until hot. Place a naan on the pan and cook for 1–2 minutes until the naan starts to puff up. Flip it over and cook the other side for 1 minute until the bubbles start to turn golden brown. Wrap in a clean kitchen towel to keep them warm and soft until you are ready to eat.

Leftover naan can be wrapped in foil and stored in an airtight container to keep them fresh for up to 2 days.

 To make garlic naan, melt 2 tablespoons of butter with 1 teaspoon of garlic paste and brush over your naan before cooking. Scatter with chopped cilantro and bake in the oven.

 These naan make a perfect base for naan pizzas—just load them up with your favorite toppings before baking!

Basmati Rice

This aromatic white rice has a delicate, fluffy texture and is the perfect accompaniment to curries and stir-fries. For perfectly cooked rice, always use a 2:1 water to rice ratio.

Ingredients

4 ounces basmati rice
1 cup water
1 bay leaf
1 cinnamon stick
½ teaspoon salt
2 tablespoons sunflower oil

Method

Wash the rice in a sieve under cold running water until the water runs clear. This will remove any excess starch, giving you more separate, fluffy grains.

Place the water in a medium saucepan over medium heat and add the bay leaf and cinnamon stick to give the rice a nice fragrance. Sprinkle the salt and pour in the oil to keep the grains from sticking together. Add the rice, cover, and cook for 10–12 minutes until the rice is tender and the liquid has been absorbed, stirring gently halfway through and making sure not to break the grains. Remove the pan from the heat, fluff up the rice with a fork, and you're ready to serve.

 TIP Add 1–2 star anise to give a sweet, aniseed-like flavor to the rice.

Tomato & Cilantro Chutney

SERVES
4

TIME
Prep: 20 minutes
Cook: 10 minutes

Sweet tomatoes and fresh cilantro really complement each other, making this chutney great with just about anything. Fill up some jars and you have a great gift just as Ramadan starts.

Ingredients

4 fresh tomatoes
1 ounce fresh cilantro leaves
4 tablespoons white vinegar
2 tablespoons lemon juice
2 teaspoons ground cumin
1 teaspoon chili powder
2 teaspoons ground black pepper
2 teaspoons garlic paste
4 tablespoons ketchup
4 tablespoons oil
2 teaspoons mustard seeds
2 teaspoons sesame seeds
6–8 curry leaves
salt

Method

Use a knife to make a shallow X on the bottom of the tomatoes, then place in a bowl of boiling water for 40–50 seconds until the skin starts to peel off easily. Skin and cut the tomatoes into quarters, then blitz in a food processor with the fresh cilantro until smooth.

Transfer to a medium saucepan with the vinegar, lemon juice, cumin, chili powder, black pepper, garlic paste, and ketchup and season with salt. Bring to a boil, then cook over low heat for 8–10 minutes until reduced and thickened. Transfer to a bowl.

Heat the oil in a small frying pan over medium heat, add the mustard seeds, sesame seeds, and curry leaves, sizzle for 30–40 seconds, then mix in to the chutney. When cool, store in the fridge for up to 7–10 days.

Pineapple Chutney

SERVES
6

TIME
Prep: 15 minutes
Cook: 40 minutes

This is the perfect sweet, spicy, and savory condiment, ideal for serving with pretty much any savory dish or snack.

Ingredients

2 pounds pineapple, peeled, cored, and chopped into chunks
2 teaspoons garlic paste
2 teaspoons ginger paste
1 teaspoon chili paste
4 tablespoons sugar
1 teaspoon ground cardamom
8–10 cloves
1 teaspoon nigella seeds
6 tablespoons white vinegar
big pinch of ground turmeric
4 tablespoons oil
2 teaspoons mustard seeds
6 dried red chilies
6–8 curry leaves
salt

Method

Place the pineapple chunks in a food processor and blitz until smooth.

Transfer to a medium saucepan with the garlic paste, ginger paste, chili paste, sugar, ground cardamom, cloves, nigella seeds, vinegar, and turmeric and season with salt. Bring to a boil, then cook over low heat for 30–40 minutes until reduced and thickened. Transfer to a bowl.

Heat the oil in a small frying pan over medium heat. Add the mustard seeds, dried chilies, and curry leaves, sizzle for 30–40 seconds, then mix in to the chutney. When cool, store in the fridge for up to 7–10 days.

Red Pepper Chutney

The sweetness from the peppers and heat from the chilies make this a fantastic accompaniment to any fried or baked appetizer such as samosas, spring rolls, or pies.

Ingredients

2 red peppers, cut into chunks
2 onions, roughly chopped
2 fresh red chilies
6–8 garlic cloves
4 tablespoons white vinegar
2 tablespoons sugar
4 tablespoons oil
2 teaspoons mustard seeds
6–8 curry leaves
salt

Method

Place the red peppers, onions, red chilies, and garlic cloves in a food processor and blitz until smooth.

Transfer to a medium saucepan with the vinegar and sugar and season with salt. Bring to a boil and cook over low heat for 8–10 minutes until reduced and thickened. Transfer to a bowl.

Heat the oil in a small frying pan over medium heat, add the mustard seeds and curry leaves, sizzle for 30–40 seconds, then mix in to the chutney. When cool, store in the fridge for up to 7–10 days.

Mint & Cilantro Yogurt Chutney

This yogurt-based chutney is very similar to raita. The fresh-tasting cilantro and zesty, fragrant mint are the perfect combo in this versatile chutney dip.

Ingredients

1 ounce fresh cilantro
1 ounce fresh mint leaves
2 fresh green chilies
4 garlic cloves
12 tablespoons plain Greek yogurt
1 teaspoon ground cumin
salt

Method

Place the cilantro, mint, chilies, and garlic in a food processor and blitz until finely chopped.

Transfer to a bowl with the yogurt and cumin, stir together, and season with salt. Store in the fridge for up to 7–10 days.

Refreshing

No one can refuse a cool and exciting colorful drink with irresistible tropical flavors, such as mango, watermelon, or lychee, or delicious creamy milkshakes like the traditional falooda, which is a must in our home. Adults and kids alike will enjoy my favorite drinks, and I really hope you make them for your own dinner parties too.

Strawberry &
Watermelon Refresher

SERVES
1

TIME
Prep: 10 minutes

Ramadan tables will usually feature watermelon—it just has to be done. It's so refreshing after a day of fasting and great for rehydration too. If you have enough, you could so easily make this cooling drink. It's colorful, tropical, and looks so good at any occasion or party. The two main ingredients complement each other so well—I hope you agree.

Ingredients

5 ounces seedless watermelon, cubed
9 ounces strawberries, hulled
1 tablespoon fresh mint leaves
1 tablespoon rose syrup
ice, to serve

Method

Place all the ingredients in a blender, saving 1 strawberry for decoration, and blitz until smooth. Serve over ice, with the strawberry to decorate.

Lemon &
Mint Mocktail

SERVES
1

TIME
Prep: 10 minutes

Such a simple idea for a drink and so easy that anyone could make it in no time at all. This smells so good and is instantly refreshing with that extra zing! Most of you should have these ingredients in your kitchen, so go ahead and make this today!

Ingredients

½ lime, thinly sliced
½ lemon, thinly sliced
1 tablespoon fresh mint leaves
1 tablespoon sugar (optional)
sparkling water, to top off
ice cubes, to serve

Method

Place the lime, lemon, and mint leaves in a tall glass and add the sugar, if using. Muddle with the tip of a wooden spoon to crush and release the oils and juices. Top off with sparkling water and add some ice cubes to serve.

Mango & Lychee Refresher

SERVES
1–2

TIME
Prep: 10 minutes

With a deliciously fresh and fruity flavor, this light and refreshing summer drink is made with nauturally sweet ingredients to jazz up your dinner table.

Ingredients

2 mangoes, peeled and sliced
6 canned lychees
1 tablespoon lime juice
1¼ cups lychee juice
ice, to serve

TO DECORATE
pomegranate seeds
lime slices

Method

Place the mangoes, lychees, and lime juice in a blender and blitz until smooth. Pour into 1 or 2 glasses over ice, top off with the lychee juice, then decorate with pomegranate seeds and lime slices.

 You could use a sparkling lychee drink or sparkling water instead of the lychee juice if you prefer, to add some bubbles and texture to your drink.

Apple Berry Mocktail

SERVES
1

TIME
Prep: 10 minutes

Apples and berries, fizzy and pretty, bold and delicious . . . what's not to like?

Ingredients

6 blackberries
6 raspberries
½ green apple, finely diced
⅔ cup apple juice
sparkling water or lemonade, to top off
ice cubes, to serve

Method

Place the blackberries, raspberries, and apple in a tall glass. Muddle with the tip of a wooden spoon to crush and release the juices. Add the apple juice, top off with sparkling water or lemonade, and add some ice cubes to serve.

Nutty Chocolate Milkshake

SERVES
1

TIME
Prep: 15 minutes

This rich and creamy milkshake will be sure to put a big smile on the face of any child or adult—and that's before you even take your first sip! Why not get your kids involved with the decoration?

Ingredients

2 scoops vanilla ice cream
1 cup milk
½ cup heavy cream
4 strawberries
6 hazelnut chocolates (I use Ferrero Rochers)

DECORATION
chocolate sauce
whipped cream
strawberries
1–2 hazelnut chocolates (I use Ferrero Rochers)

Method

Place the ice cream in a blender with the milk, heavy cream, strawberries, and chocolates and blend until smooth.

Drizzle some chocolate sauce inside a tall glass for decoration before pouring in the milkshake. Top with whipped cream and decorate with strawberries and extra whole chocolates.

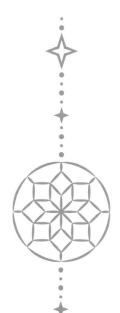

Sweet Yogurt Lassi

SERVES
2

TIME
Prep: 10 minutes

Sweet Lassi is a yogurt-based beverage, sweetened with sugar and flavored with cardamom. It's a popular drink that is usually served with rice dishes, such as pilau and biryani. Every time I make biryani, I always have to make lassi, as my children will not have biryani without it.

Ingredients

1⅔ cups plain or Greek yogurt
3 tablespoons sugar
¼ teaspoon ground cardamom
about ¼ cup milk

Method

Place all the ingredients in a large pitcher and mix well with a hand whisk for 1–2 minutes until nice and frothy. Add a little extra milk if it's too thick for you. Pour into 2 glasses and serve with your biryani.

 TIP For Sweet & Sour Lassi, add a little green chili paste to the drink. Then you get the best of both worlds!

Falooda

SERVES
2

TIME
Prep: 45 minutes
Cook: 20 minutes
Chill: 1 hour

This traditional, ultimate Indian drink has exciting layers of flavor and textures and is the beverage of choice on any iftar table at the end of a fasting day, or any day for that matter. It has a creamy flavor, delicately perfumed with rose, and a nice dollop of ice cream to make it extra cooling. It's quite a major part of Middle Eastern and Indian culture, from the villages of the subcontinent to homes here in the United States! It looks so pretty and exotic in pink, don't you think?

Ingredients

½ teaspoon basil seeds (tukmaria)
½ cup water
2 cups whole milk
2 tablespoons sugar
2 tablespoons heavy cream
½ teaspoon ground cardamom
2 tablespoons rose syrup, plus extra to decorate
2 tablespoons falooda vermicelli, soaked in water
   to soften
2 scoops of vanilla ice cream
1 teaspoon chopped pistachios and almonds

FALOODA JELLY
½ cup water
1 teaspoon falooda powder
1–2 drops pink food coloring

Method

For the falooda jelly, place the water, falooda powder, and pink food coloring in a small saucepan over medium heat and bring to a boil. Pour into a heatproof dish and leave to set until firm.

Soak the basil seeds in the water for 30 minutes—they will start to swell. Drain through a tea strainer to remove excess water and set aside.

Pour the milk into a large saucepan over medium heat and bring to a boil. Add the sugar and boil for 1 minute, stirring all the time so that the milk doesn't stick to the pan and burn. Once boiled, cool and chill in the fridge for 1 hour.

Add the cream and ground cardamom to the chilled milk and whisk together. Grate the falooda jelly using a coarse grater.

Divide the rose syrup between 2 tall glasses and add the soaked vermicelli and basil seeds. Pour in the milk, which will change the color to a subtle pink. Add 1 tablespoon of grated falooda jelly to each glass, then top with the ice cream and chopped nuts and drizzle a little rose syrup on top to decorate.

 TIP Rose syrup can be quite sweet, so adjust the amount of sugar you add to the milk accordingly.

 TIP If you are short on time, you don't have to boil the milk, but it does give the falooda a richer, thicker, and creamier taste.

EVERYTHING

Sweet

Everyone who knows me is well aware that I have a sweet tooth. Here I have some oh-so-indulgent desserts for you to enjoy in Ramadan after a day of fasting—or for any celebration for that matter! There are light and airy desserts and sweet treats to enjoy with a good cup of tea. You'll be sure to find something you and your family will absolutely fall in love with.

Lemon & Cardamom Cupcakes

SERVES

2

TIME

Prep: 40 minutes
Cook: 20 minutes

These cupcakes are super-moist, light, and fluffy—bursting with zesty, zingy lemon, with cardamom adding a sweet, spicy aroma. This is my favorite combo in a cupcake.

Ingredients

9 tablespoons butter or margarine at room temperature
½ cup superfine sugar
1 cup self-rising flour
½ teaspoon baking powder
2 eggs
1 tablespoon milk
2 tablespoons lemon juice
1 teaspoon finely grated lemon zest
½ teaspoon ground cardamom, plus extra to decorate

LEMON CREAM
1¼ cups heavy cream
2–3 heaping tablespoons lemon curd

Method

Preheat the oven to 325°F and line a 12-cup muffin tin with paper cases.

Place all the cake ingredients in a bowl and mix everything together with a hand mixer until just smooth, making sure not to overmix. Divide the mixture equally among the cupcake cases and cook in the oven for 18–20 minutes until they are golden brown and spring back when pressed. Leave the cupcakes to cool completely on a wire rack.

To make the lemon cream, pour the cream into a large bowl, add the lemon curd, and mix until soft peaks form. Fill a piping bag with a closed star nozzle and pipe the cream on the cupcakes to form a swirl. Sprinkle a little ground cardamom on top to finish off.

Any leftover cream-topped cupcakes can be stored in the fridge for up to 3 days.

Mango Falooda Dessert

SERVES
9–10

TIME
Prep: 25 minutes
Cook: 20 minutes
Chill: 3 hours

Dessert is a must for iftar during Ramadan in our house. Whether it's ice cream, Jell-O, or fresh fruits, something sweet is on the table to enjoy after the main meal. I normally make a rose version of this dessert, but this Mango Falooda is just as delicious—I absolutely love mangoes. This dessert is so creamy, soft, and light and totally melts in your mouth.

Ingredients

4¼ cups milk
2 tablespoons custard powder
2 tablespoons milk powder
2½ teaspoons falooda powder
14 ounces canned mango pulp
6 tablespoons heavy cream
7 ounces condensed milk
¼ teaspoon ground cardamom

DECORATION
mango chunks
pomegranate seeds
chopped pistachios
pinch of saffron threads

Method

Set aside ⅔ cup of the milk and pour the rest into a large saucepan over low heat. Heat gently until the milk starts to simmer—this may take up to 20 minutes. Keep an eye on the milk and give it an occasional stir.

Place the reserved milk in a pitcher with the custard powder, milk powder, and falooda powder and mix until smooth. Add this mixture to the hot milk and stir over gentle heat. You will notice the milk will start to thicken. With the heat still on low, add the mango pulp, heavy cream, condensed milk, and ground cardamom and mix everything to combine.

Pour into individual dessert bowls or into a large dish, allow to cool, then chill in the fridge for 3 hours to set. Decorate with mango chunks, pomegranate seeds, chopped pistachios, and a few saffron threads before serving.

This dessert will happily keep in the fridge for 1–2 days, so you can prepare it ahead of time and decorate it just before serving.

 TIP Falooda is a setting agent, sometimes called agar-agar or China grass.

Saffron Nan Khatai

MAKES
30

TIME
Prep: 30 minutes
Cook: 12 minutes

Nan khatai is a traditional Indian shortbread and my absolute favorite! When I was growing up, my mum would make a huge batch of these for Eid—the aroma of freshly baked Nan Khatai would fill the house. The name comes from the Persian word "naan," which means "bread," and "khatai," means "light and flaky." Typically made with ghee, flour, sugar, and cardamom, these are crisp and crumbly on the outside with a slight chewiness in the middle. A perfect sweet treat for special occasions.

Ingredients

½ cup superfine sugar
⅔ cup ghee
4 tablespoons oil
1 teaspoon saffron threads
1 teaspoon ground cardamom
1 tablespoon fine semolina
4 ounces ground almonds
1 tablespoon chickpea flour
½ teaspoon baking powder
¼ teaspoon baking soda
about 1¼ cups all-purpose flour

DECORATION
candied cherries
chopped almonds
pistachios
dried rose petals

Method

Preheat the oven to 325°F and line a baking sheet with parchment paper.

Place the sugar and ghee in a bowl and use a whisk to cream them together for 2–3 minutes until light and fluffy. Add the oil and whisk for a further 40 seconds.

Place the saffron threads in a small frying pan over very low heat and warm through, taking care as the strands burn easily. When slightly crisp, crush with the back of a spoon and add to the creamed mixture with the ground cardamom to give both aromatic and sweet spicy flavor.

Add the semolina and ground almonds to provide a crunchy and crisp texture, and the chickpea flour for a slighty nutty taste. Add the baking powder and baking soda to add a little rise and some cracks on top of the shortbread during baking—that's when you know you have a good nan khatai. Finally, add just enough flour to make a soft and pliable dough.

Roll the dough into small balls, about 1½ inches across, and place on the prepared baking sheet, spacing them a little apart as they do spread during baking. Decorate them with candied cherries, chopped almonds, pistachios, or dried rose petals, then cook in the oven for 12 minutes. They will crack slightly on top as they bake and turn lightly golden brown. Leave to cool on the baking sheet for 5 minutes to firm up slightly, then cool completely on a wire rack. Store in an airtight container in a cool place for up to 2–3 weeks.

School Dinner Cake

SERVES
25

TIME
Prep: 30 minutes
Cook: 30 minutes

This retro vanilla sheet cake is an easy bake for celebrations and parties, and it brings back fond memories of school. I remember rushing in at lunchtime to join the line for a slice of this, devouring each and every crumb. The sponge is incredibly fluffy and soft, the simple icing gives it just the right amount of sweetness, and the rainbow sprinkles add that pop of color. This one is definitely a crowd-pleaser.

Ingredients

16 tablespoons (2 sticks) butter or margarine at room temperature
1¾ cups superfine sugar
4 eggs, beaten
1 teaspoon vanilla extract
2 cups self-rising flour
1 teaspoon baking powder
3 tablespoons milk
rainbow sprinkles, to decorate

GLACÉ ICING

1⅓ cups confectioners' sugar
2–3 tablespoons milk
1 teaspoon vanilla extract (optional)

Method

Preheat the oven to 325°F and grease and line an 8-inch square cake pan with parchment paper.

Cream the butter and sugar together in a bowl until light and fluffy using a hand mixer or wooden spoon. Beat in the eggs and stir in the vanilla extract. Fold in the flour and baking powder with a large metal spoon, then add the milk to create a smooth batter, taking care not to overmix.

Transfer the mixture to the prepared cake pan and gently spread out with a spatula. Cook in the oven for 25–30 minutes until golden brown and coming away from the edges of the pan. A skewer inserted into the middle should come out clean.

Set aside to cool in the pan for 5 minutes, then turn out, peel off the paper, and transfer to a wire rack to cool completely.

For the glacé icing, sift the confectioners' sugar into a bowl and gradually add the milk, a little at a time, until the icing becomes thick enough to coat the back of a spoon. If necessary, adjust the consistency with a few drops more milk or a little more confectioners' sugar. The icing should be smooth and glossy. Add the vanilla, if using, then pour the icing on the cooled cake, using a spoon to guide it to the edges. Finish off with rainbow sprinkles.

Allow the icing to set, then cut the cake into 1½-inch squares. Store any leftover cake in an airtight container for up to 3–4 days.

Phirni Rice Dessert

SERVES

5

TIME

Prep: 15 minutes
Cook: 20 minutes
Setting: 1–2 hours

Phirni is a classic Indian dessert, so light and creamy and made with just a few simple ingredients. I remember making this with my grandmother during Ramadan—the aroma while the mixture started to bubble, pouring out the mixture into small bowls, then setting them to chill in the fridge, ready just in time for iftar.

Ingredients

2½ cups whole milk
4 tablespoons rice flour
½ teaspoon rose extract
3–4 tablespoons granulated sugar
1 tablespoon shredded coconut
½ teaspoon ground cardamom

Method

Place the milk, rice flour, rose extract, and sugar in a large saucepan over medium heat. Bring the mixture to a boil, stirring all the time so it doesn't get lumpy or stick to the pan. This can take about 20 minutes. The consistency should be thick like pudding.

Pour into small dessert bowls, sprinkle with the coconut and ground cardamom, and pop into the fridge to set for 1–2 hours. Serve chilled.

Pink Lamingtons

MAKES
25

TIME
Prep: 45 minutes
Cook: 30 minutes

Scrumptiously soft and fluffy sponge cake, dipped in Jell-O and coated in shredded coconut, these pretty pink sponge squares are something I make every Eid to share with family and friends. You can dress them up with a bit of buttercream and a dollop of jam or have them just as they are.

Ingredients

16 tablespoons (2 sticks) butter or margarine at room temperature
1¾ cups superfine sugar
4 eggs, beaten
1 teaspoon vanilla extract
2 cups self-rising flour
1 teaspoon baking powder
3 tablespoons milk
7 ounces shredded coconut
raspberry jam, for filling

JELL-O ICING
2½ ounces raspberry or strawberry gelatin crystals (I recommend Ahmed Foods brand)
1⅔ cups boiling water (or as much needed to create the consistency of cream)
2 tablespoons confectioners' sugar

BUTTERCREAM
11 tablespoons butter at room temperature
1⅓ cups confectioners' sugar
½ teaspoon vanilla extract
1 tablespoon milk (optional)

Method

Preheat the oven to 325°F and grease and line an 8-inch square cake pan with parchment paper.

Cream the butter and sugar together in a bowl until light and fluffy using a hand mixer or wooden spoon. Beat in the eggs and stir in the vanilla extract. Fold in the flour and baking powder with a large metal spoon, then add the milk to create a smooth batter, taking care not to overmix.

Transfer the mixture to the prepared cake pan and gently spread out with a spatula. Cook in the oven for 25–30 minutes until golden brown and coming away from the edges of the pan. A toothpick inserted into the middle should come out clean.

Set aside to cool in the pan for 5 minutes, then turn out, peel off the paper, and transfer to a wire rack to cool completely.

For the Jell-O icing, dissolve the gelatin crystals by gradually adding boiling water in a shallow bowl until the mixture reaches the consistency of cream. Then add the confectioners' sugar and stir until dissolved. Place the shredded coconut in another shallow bowl.

Cut the cake into 1½-inch squares and dip each piece into the Jell-O icing to cover, then toss in the coconut to coat. Place the coated cakes on a wire rack over a tray to allow any excess icing to drip away and leave to set.

For the buttercream, beat all the ingredients together for 3–4 minutes until soft and creamy, adding the milk if the buttercream is too thick. Place the buttercream in a piping bag fitted with a star nozzle.

Cut the lamingtons in half, spread with a layer of raspberry jam, pipe buttercream on top, and sandwich them back together.

Store in an airtight container for up to 2–3 days at room temperature or a week in the fridge.

 The lamingtons can also be filled with whipped cream if you prefer.

Gulab Jamun

Gulab Jamun is a classic Indian sweet treat enjoyed at all celebratory occasions. These soft syrup-soaked balls are an absolute delight and will surely satisfy your sweet cravings.

Ingredients

7 ounces condensed milk
1½ tablespoons plain yogurt
1 egg yolk
1½ tablespoons ghee
2 tablespoons fine semolina
½ teaspoon ground cardamom
1 cup all-purpose flour
½ cup self-rising flour
1½ teaspoons baking powder
oil, for deep-frying
4 ounces shredded coconut

SUGAR SYRUP
1¼ cups granulated sugar
1 cup water
½ teaspoon rose extract

Method

For the sugar syrup, place all the ingredients in large saucepan over medium heat and cook until the sugar dissolves. This could take 20 minutes. Reduce the heat and simmer gently until the syrup turns slightly sticky. Set aside.

Place the condensed milk in a bowl with the yogurt, egg yolk, ghee, semolina, and ground cardamom and mix it all together. Sift in the all-purpose flour, self-rising flour, and baking powder and bring together into a soft dough.

Divide the dough into 28 equal-sized balls and roll each in the palms of your hands into an oval shape about 1½ inches long.

Heat the oil for deep-frying in a large saucepan over medium-low heat. Lower a few jamun into the oil at a time and fry for about 2 minutes, making sure not to crowd the pan because they will increase in size. It's important to fry the jamuns on low heat—if the oil is too hot, the jamuns will brown on the outside and stay raw in the middle. Keep stirring gently to fry them evenly so they are golden brown all over.

Carefully remove from the oil with a slotted spoon, drain well, and place in the saucepan with the warm sugar syrup. Leave to soak in the syrup for about 1 minute, then remove them and toss in shredded coconut to coat.

Store in an airtight container in the fridge for up to 3–4 days.

Rose & Pistachio Milk Cake

SERVES
6–7

TIME
Prep: 35 minutes
Cook: 25 minutes
Resting 3 hours

Also known as Rose & Pistachio Tres Leches or Three-Milk Cake, this is the perfect dessert to pretty up your table. Trust me, it's so easy, tastes absolutely heavenly, and looks so good. This is an incredibly indulgent, sophisticated, and moreish dessert, and you just can't say no to it!

Ingredients

4 eggs, separated
¾ cup granulated sugar
2 tablespoons rose syrup
3 tablespoons milk
1⅓ cups self-rising flour
½ teaspoon baking powder
½ teaspoon ground cardamom

ROSE MILK

14.5 ounces evaporated milk
1 cup whole milk
1 cup heavy whipping cream
5 ounces condensed milk
1 tablespoon rose syrup
pinch of ground cardamom

TOPPING

1½ cups heavy whipping cream
1–2 tablespoons rose syrup
chopped pistachios
dried rose petals
pinch of ground cardamom

Method

Preheat the oven to 350°F and line an 11-by-7-inch shallow heatproof dish with parchment paper.

Place the egg yolks in a large bowl with half the sugar and whisk with a hand mixer on medium speed until thick and pale in color. Mix in the rose syrup—this will instantly change the color of the mixture and give an amazing flavor to the sponge. Add the milk and sift in the flour and baking powder. Add the ground cardamom and gently fold in until just combined.

Place the egg whites in another large bowl with the remaining sugar. Clean and dry the beaters, then beat the egg whites until stiff peaks form. Carefully fold the egg whites into the egg yolk mixture until fully combined, taking care not to knock out too much of the air.

Pour the mixture into the prepared dish and cook in the oven for 25 minutes, or until the sponge is golden brown, and springs back when pressed.

For the rose milk, mix all the ingredients together in a pitcher. Use a skewer to poke holes all over the cake, then slowly pour most of the milk mixture over the top, reserving a little for serving. Refrigerate for a few hours or overnight to allow the cake to soak up the milk.

For the topping, beat the cream and rose syrup together until soft peaks form, then

spread on the cake. Decorate with
chopped pistachios, rose petals, and a
sprinkling of ground cardamom. Cut the
cake into squares and serve with the
remaining rose milk.

Store in an airtight container in the fridge
for up to 3–4 days.

My Desi Pantry

These are the most commonly used ingredients in Indian cooking and in this book.

◗ Bay leaves

Usually added at the beginning of cooking, they release flavor and infuse the dish with a floral and herbal scent.

◗ Black peppercorns

Woody and pungent, used in most savory dishes, ground or whole.

◗ Cardamom (*elaichi*)

With an earthy, bittersweet taste and aroma, cardamom is used in both sweet and savory dishes. It comes in both whole (pod) and powdered (ground) forms. For curries and rice dishes, it's typical to use cardamom pods, but ground cardamom is great for sweet dishes or desserts.

◗ Carom seeds (*ajwain*)

Little seeds with a pungent, sharp, herby taste and smell.

◗ Cassava

A root vegetable with a subtle taste that is slightly sweet, earthy, and nutty. Tastes amazing when cooked with strongly flavored ingredients. I tend to use frozen cassava, as it's much more convenient, but if you can find fresh in your local supermarket or street market, that tastes even better.

◗ Chickpea flour (*besan, gram flour*)

Perfect for making batter, especially for deep-frying. Commonly used to make pakoras.

◗ Chili paste (*lila mircha*)

Adds a kick and a fresh flavor to your dishes. I like to make my own paste by blitzing fresh chilies in a food processor, but you can also buy jars of chili paste, which will work just as well.

◗ Chili powder (*lal mircha*)

A key ingredient in many Indian dishes, adding heat to your food. Adjust the quantity according to your or your family's preference.

◗ Chilies, fresh (*lila mircha*)

There's a huge variety of chilies available to buy. My family always used bird's eye chilies, so these are the ones I always have ready to use. They have a nice level of heat. I like to use a mix of red and green ones in my cooking. However, for garnishes, I'll use jalapeños because they're normally less spicy.

Cilantro, fresh (lila dhania)

A fresh leafy herb with a fragrant, citrus flavor, perfect as a garnish for many dishes. Adds freshness to appetizers and curries.

Cinnamon (tuj)

Available as sticks or in ground form, cinnamon is the bark of a tree and has a sweet flavor and woody fragrance; used in both savory and sweet dishes.

Cloves (laung)

Sweet, warm, woody, and fragrant, cloves are added to curries and rice dishes.

Coriander, ground (dhania)

A key ingredient in many Indian dishes with its fresh-tasting, lemony flavor, it is mildly sweet and aromatic; often added to curries, rice dishes, and appetizers.

Cumin, ground (jeera)

Another key ingredient in many Indian dishes. It has a warm, earthy, and bittersweet taste and is used frequently in curries, rice dishes, and appetizers.

Curry leaves (kaddi patta)

Most often sizzled (tempered) first in oil to release their natural flavors and sweet pungent aroma, curry leaves appear in many dishes.

Dill, fresh

A grass-like herb, slightly tangy and often used in seafood dishes, sauces, and soups. Used in limited quantities to avoid overpowering a dish.

Fenugreek leaves (kasturi methi)

Slightly bitter, earthy leaves used to enhance flavor and aroma. Available fresh or dried.

Falooda powder (agar-agar, China grass)

A thickening or setting agent used as a vegetarian substitute for gelatin in desserts and puddings.

Fennel seeds (saunf)

Green seeds with an aniseed-like flavor and warm sweet aroma; used in sweet and savory dishes.

Garam masala

A warm, fragrant spice blend used in rice and curries. Used in limited quantities to avoid overpowering a dish.

Garlic

A key ingredient in many Indian dishes. When raw it has an intense, pungent, and unique flavor and aroma, but after cooking it mellows down and is mild and sweet. If you have time, nothing beats using fresh garlic cloves, either crushed or finely chopped. However, if you don't have time for this, you can buy jars of chopped garlic that are brilliant.

Ghee (clarified butter)

With its rich, nutty, and buttery flavor, ghee can be used in sweet or savory dishes. If you can't find ghee, use unsalted butter instead.

Ginger

A key ingredient in many Indian dishes, ginger is so versatile and can be added to curries, rice, appetizers, and beverages. Ginger has a pungent, spicy aroma and zingy taste. As with garlic, if you have time, fresh ginger will have more flavor; however, jarred versions can work just as well. Few recipes for Ramadan use ground ginger, so this type of ginger doesn't feature much.

Kashmiri chili powder

A mild chili powder with a bright red color.

Mango powder (*amchor*)

Dried, ground mango, adding a sour, tangy, and slightly sweet undertone to dishes.

Mint, fresh

A highly aromatic herb with a subtle, sweet taste, adding a cool freshness to your dishes.

Mustard seeds

Little round seeds with a pungent, nutty taste, typically used when tempering.

Nigella seeds (*kalonji*)

Also known as black onion seeds, these are strong, nutty, and have a slightly bitter aroma. They are often added to curries and rice dishes or as a garnish.

Onions

A key ingredient for most dishes and a staple vegetable in Indian cooking. With their pungent, punchy, sharp flavor, and strong distinct smell, onions are the perfect base for all curries, adding texture to the sauce.

Paneer

Similar to cottage cheese, paneer has a milky, creamy flavor. It is bland in taste but perfect for recipes with spices, as it absorbs all the flavors.

Paprika

A ground spice made from a mixture of dried peppers. The flavor can be anything from sweet and mild to spicy and hot. It adds a bright reddish color and a pleasant pepper aroma.

Peri-peri seasoning

A sour, sweet, and salty blend of spices, perfect for marinating.

Rice flour

A good thickening agent for soups, rice flour is finer than wheat flour. It is often used in fried foods or tempura batter to coat seafood, chicken, or vegetables, and the results are crispy, weightless, and tender.

Saffron (*kesar*)

The brilliant yellow stamens of a crocus, saffron adds color and aroma to both sweet and savory dishes. When possible, try to use threads of saffron instead of powder—they're higher quality and so give a better flavor.

Samosa leaves (samosa pastry, *pur*)

Available in packages, samosa leaves are rectangles of thin pastry used to make samosas—they become very crispy when fried. They can be found in most Indian grocery stores. You'll need to look in the freezer section for these, as they are only available frozen.

Semolina (*sooji*)

Semolina flour has a slightly nutty, sweet taste and a coarse texture. It is used in sweet and savory dishes.

Sesame seeds (*tal*)

Oval-shaped white seeds with a mild, sweet, nutty taste. Great as a garnish or sprinkled on savory dishes and snacks.

Star anise

Pretty star-shaped seed pods with a slightly sweet aroma and flavor like aniseed or licorice.

Tandoori masala

A strong red spice mixture, adding a lovely vibrant color and warm spicy flavor to your dishes.

Tomatoes, fresh or canned

Tomatoes are essential in making the masala base for many curries, making the dish saucy and adding a tangy sweetness. In the recipes, I've specified when it's best to use fresh or canned (and sometimes use both!). This is because each type gives a different flavor, texture, and color to the dish.

Turmeric, ground (*arad, haldi*)

A key ingredient in many Indian dishes, ground turmeric is the dried and powdered root of a plant in the ginger family. It adds an immediate, intense, mustardy yellow color to your dishes. Used in limited quantities.

My Favorite Spice Mixes

···◆···

I love to have some of my favorite and most used spice blends ready to go in my cupboard to save time when I'm cooking. All these mixes use spices you can easily find in your local supermarket, and if you double or even triple the quantities below, they'll keep in an airtight container for months.

I use these mixes for several recipes in this book, but they're also great as a rub on some vegetables that you're panfrying, or on meats that you're barbecuing or grilling. You can even cook the spices for a couple of minutes in some oil in a pan, and then add to cooked rice and leftover veggies for a quick, simple meal that's packed with flavor.

Perfect Curry Spice Mix

This is a brilliant spice blend for a simply delicious curry. It's really versatile, so I always have a pot ready-made in my cupboard.

1 teaspoon chili powder
1 teaspoon ground cumin
1 teaspoon ground coriander
1 teaspoon ground black pepper
½ teaspoon ground turmeric
½ teaspoon garam masala
½ teaspoon salt

Meat Biryani Masala

This masala is slightly different from the veggie one, but that means it goes well with meat dishes. Chicken, beef, and lamb are our favorites.

1 tablespoon chili powder
1 teaspoon ground black pepper
½ teaspoon ground cardamom
½ teaspoon garam masala
1 tablespoon ground cumin
1 tablespoon ground coriander

Bhuna Masala

Bhuna is a dry curry with a medium-hot heat. This is the perfect spice blend for any type of bhuna.

1 tablespoon ground cumin
2 tablespoons ground coriander
1 tablespoon Kashmiri chili powder
1 tablespoon chili flakes
1 teaspoon ground turmeric
1 teaspoon nigella seeds
1 teaspoon dried fenugreek leaves
1 tablespoon ground black pepper
1 tablespoon store-bought tandoori masala
1 teaspoon salt

Vegetable Biryani Masala

"Masala" here simply means a mixture of spices. This one is perfect for vegetable-based dishes.

2 teaspoons chili powder
1 teaspoon Kashmiri chili powder
1 tablespoon ground coriander
1 tablespoon ground cumin
½ teaspoon garam masala
1 teaspoon salt
½ teaspoon ground turmeric

Reader Recipes

Ramadan is all about community, so I wanted to leave some space for you to write in your own beloved recipes— maybe ones passed down to you from your parents or grandparents, or a new favorite that you've discovered from friends or online. Write them here so you can keep them safe and maybe even pass them on to the next generation!

NAME

SERVES

TIME

Ingredients

Method

Ingredients

Method

Ingredients

Method

Ingredients

Method

Ingredients

Method

Ingredients

Method

Ingredients

Method

Ingredients

Method

Ingredients

Method

Ingredients

Method

SERVES

TIME

Ingredients

Method

Ingredients

Method

Ingredients

Method

Ingredients

Method

Acknowledgments

First and foremost, I would like to thank The Almighty, who has given me strength and encouragement, endless love, continuous blessings, and guidance throughout my life.

My beloved gran and mum for motivating and inspiring me in my younger days, when my passion for food started, and teaching me the basic culinary skills, without which my kitchen experience wouldn't be where it is today.

I am eternally grateful to my dad, who taught me discipline, manners, respect, and so much more that has helped me in life.

My lovely mother-in-law for giving me the ability to continue my cooking journey where it left off, sharing her techniques with me, supporting and inspiring me, helping me experiment with different recipe ideas in the kitchen.

My dear father-in-law for always encouraging me to keep pushing forward and to never say no to any opportunities that come my way, for being there for us, and offering words of wisdom.

Special thanks to our beautiful daughter for actually taking the time to try out and follow some of the recipes, giving honest feedback, and offering a helping hand to make my life a little easier.

Our darling two boys for taking charge of the tasting sessions, having an interest in what I'm doing and giving opinions, and for always cheering me up and making me smile.

My super-awesome management team, Umarah, Reza, Omar, and Saif, for always looking after my interests; always being helpful; handling day-to-day communications, campaigns, and projects; and generally being there for me.

Thank you to Ru for recognizing my work, having faith in me to deliver this book, caring and guiding me throughout the process; and also to Sam and Jo for working with me to create something special, making the book look perfect for readers to enjoy. And of course, not forgetting the photographers and stylists for making the book look so beautiful inside and out, and everyone else behind the scenes for helping me make my dream come true.

Thank you to everyone who supports me and my journey.

My biggest thanks has to go to my amazing husband, Adam, who has been with me on this journey since day one, always being the most supportive person in my life every step of the way, motivating me to never give up, keeping it real with me, and having confidence in me even if sometimes I doubted myself. Thank you for always being my rock!

Index

A

achari kheema 70
almonds
    date & nut slices 15
    falooda 147
    saffron nan khatai 155
apple berry mocktail 141
atta flour
    roti 126–7
    saucy gazebo chicken 84

B

bananas
    banana, date & oat smoothie 16
    caramelized bananas on brioche toast 12
beef
    beef bhuna 118
    spicy beef 82
beef, ground
    beef kheema pilau 104–5
    beef kofta curry 112–13
bhuna masala 169
biryani
    lamb biryani 115–16
    veggie biryani 102–3
blackberries
    apple berry mocktail 141
Bombay potatoes 62
bread
    caramelized bananas on brioche toast 12
    chicken bread rolls 50–1
    lamb & mint buns 40–1
    see also flatbread
bread crumbs
    beef kofta curry 112–13
    chicken bread rolls 50–1
    chicken croquettes 35
    jalapeño & chicken samosas 32–3
butter chicken 67

C

cabbage
    chicken chow mein 79
    Chinese-style spring rolls 47
    egg-fried rice 81
    vegetable noodles 89
cake
    lemon & cardamom cupcakes 150
    pink lamingtons 158–9
    rose & pistachio milk cake 162–3
    school dinner cake 156
caramelized bananas on brioche toast 12
cardamom
    lemon & cardamom cupcakes 150
carrots
    chicken chow mein 79
    Chinese-style spring rolls 47
    creamy mixed vegetables 63
    egg-fried rice 81
    vegetable karahi 108
    vegetable noodles 89
cashews
    date & nut slices 15
cassava
    chicken, cassava & corn casserole 69
    paneer & cassava sizzler 87
casseroles
    chicken, cassava & corn casserole 69
cauliflower Manchurian 93
chana chaat 125
Cheddar
    cheesy chicken muffins 20
    jalapeño & chicken samosas 32–3
    veggie pizza pinwheels 48
cheesy chicken muffins 20
chicken
    butter chicken 67
    cheesy chicken muffins 20
    chicken, cassava & corn casserole 69
    chicken & piccalilli squares 28–9
    chicken & potato curry 117
    chicken Balti 98
    chicken bread rolls 50–1
    chicken chow mein 79
    chicken croquettes 35
    hariyali chicken 42
    jalapeño & chicken samosas 32–3
    masala roast chicken & herby potatoes 72

orange chili chicken 95
saucy gazebo chicken 84
sweet & sour chicken 88
chickpea flour
    crispy pakoras 45
    khuri & khitchri 56–7
    saffron nan khatai 155
    salmon pakoras 46
chickpeas
    chana chaat 125
chili
    orange chili chicken 95
Chinese-style spring rolls 47
chow mein
    chicken chow mein 79
chutneys
    mint & cilantro yogurt chutney 137
    pineapple chutney 136
    red pepper chutney 137
    tomato & cilantro chutney 133
cilantro
    mint & cilantro yogurt chutney 137
    tomato & cilantro chutney 133
classic kachumbar salad 122
coconut, creamed
    chicken, cassava & corn casserole 69
coconut, shredded
    gulab jamun 161
    phirni rice dessert 157
    pink lamingtons 158–9
condensed milk
    gulab jamun 161
    mango falooda dessert 152
    rose & pistachio milk cake 162–3
corn, canned
    cheesy chicken muffins 20
    chicken bread rolls 50–1
    crispy pakoras 45
    egg-fried rice 81
    spicy potato & corn tortilla samosas 26
    vegetable karahi 108
    veggie pizza pinwheels 48
    see also corn on the cob
corn on the cob
    chicken, cassava & corn casserole 69
    creamy mixed vegetables 63
    see also corn, canned
cream
    butter chicken 67
    chicken croquettes 35
    creamy mixed vegetables 63
    falooda 147
    khuri & khitchri 56–7
    lemon & cardamom cupcakes 150
    mango falooda dessert 152
    nutty chocolate milkshake 144
    rose & pistachio milk cake 162–3
cream cheese
    chicken bread rolls 50–1

jalapeño & chicken samosas 32–3
creamy mixed vegetables 63
crispy pakoras 45
croquettes
    chicken croquettes 35
cucumber
    classic kachumbar salad 122
curries
    beef bhuna 118
    beef kofta curry 112–13
    chicken & potato curry 117
    chicken Balti 98
    khuri & khitchri 56–7
    kidney bean curry 68
    king prawn & fish curry 111
    naan gosht 100–1
    vegetable karahi 108

D

dates
    banana, date & oat smoothie 16
    date & nut slices 15
desserts
    gulab jamun 161
    mango falooda dessert 152
    phirni rice dessert 157
dhoodi (bottle gourd)
    vegetable karahi 108
drinks
    apple berry mocktail 141
    banana, date & oat smoothie 16
    falooda 147
    lemon & mint mocktail 140
    mango & lychee refresher 141
    nutty chocolate milkshake 144
    strawberry & watermelon refresher 140
    sweet yogurt lassi 145
drumsticks (moringa)
    vegetable karahi 108
dynamite prawns 39

E

eggplant
    veggie biryani 102–3
    vegetable karahi 108
eggs
    egg-fried rice 81
    folded omelet with cherry tomatoes & feta 17
    fried eggs with peppers & za'atar 23
    shakshuka 19
evaporated milk
    rose & pistachio milk cake 162–3

F

falooda
  falooda 147
  mango falooda dessert 152
feta
  folded omelet with cherry tomatoes & feta 17
  watermelon, feta & mint salad 124
fish
  king prawn & fish curry 111
  peri-peri sea bass 106
  salmon pakoras 46
flatbread
  naan 130–1
  roti 126–7
fried eggs with peppers & za'atar 23

G

green beans
  egg-fried rice 81
  vegetable noodles 89
green peppers
  cauliflower Manchurian 93
  chicken Balti 98
  chicken bread rolls 50–1
  chicken chow mein 79
  Chinese-style spring rolls 47
  egg-fried rice 81
  fried eggs with peppers & za'atar 23
  jalapeño & chicken samosas 32–3
  keema pies 36–7
  lamb biryani 115–16
  paneer & cassava sizzler 87
  prawn jalfrezi 64
  saucy gazebo chicken 84
  spicy beef 82
  sweet & sour chicken 88
  sweet & sour prawns 77
  veggie biryani 102–3
  vegetable karahi 108
  vegetable noodles 89
  veggie pizza pinwheels 48
gulab jamun 161

H

haleem
  lamb haleem 54
hariyali chicken 42

I

ice cream
  falooda 147
  nutty chocolate milkshake 144

J

jalapeño & chicken samosas 32–3
jalfrezi
  prawn jalfrezi 64

K

keema pies 36–7
khuri & khitchri 56–7
kidney beans
  kidney bean curry 68
king prawns
  dynamite prawns 39
  king prawn & fish curry 111
  prawn jalfrezi 64
  sweet & sour prawns 77

L

lamb
  lamb & mint buns 40–1
  lamb biryani 115–16
  lamb haleem 54
  lamb stir-fry 90
  naan gosht 100–1
  sizzling lamb steaks 61
  sticky lamb chops 80
lamb, ground
  achari kheema 70
  keema pies 36–7
  lamb & mint buns 40–1
lemon
  lemon & cardamom cupcakes 150
  lemon & mint mocktail 140
lime
  lemon & mint mocktail 140
  mango & lychee refresher 141
lychee
  mango & lychee refresher 141

M

mango & lychee refresher 141
mango falooda dessert 152
masala roast chicken & herby potatoes 72
mayonnaise
    spicy mayo sauce 39
meat biryani masala 169
milk
    banana, date & oat smoothie 16
    butter chicken 67
    falooda 147
    khuri & khitchri 56–7
    mango falooda dessert 152
    nutty chocolate milkshake 144
    phirni rice dessert 157
    rose & pistachio milk cake 162–3
mint
    lamb & mint buns 40–1
    lemon & mint mocktail 140
    mint & cilantro yogurt chutney 137
    watermelon, feta & mint salad 124
mozzarella
    spicy potato & corn tortilla samosas 26
muffins
    cheesy chicken muffins 20

N

naan 130–1
naan gosht 100–1
noodles
    chicken chow mein 79
    Chinese-style spring rolls 47
    lamb stir-fry 90
    vegetable noodles 89
nutty chocolate milkshake 144

O

oats
    banana, date & oat smoothie 16
olives
    veggie pizza pinwheels 48
    watermelon, feta & mint salad 124
omelet
    folded omelet with cherry tomatoes & feta 17
onions
    achari kheema 70
    beef bhuna 118
    beef kheema pilau 104–5
    beef kofta curry 112–13
    butter chicken 67
    chicken, cassava & corn casserole 69
    chicken & piccalilli squares 28–9
    chicken & potato curry 117
    chicken Balti 98
    chicken bread rolls 50–1
    chicken chow mein 79
    Chinese-style spring rolls 47
    crispy pakoras 45
    egg-fried rice 81
    jalapeño & chicken samosas 32–3
    keema pies 36–7
    khuri & khitchri 56–7
    kidney bean curry 68
    king prawn & fish curry 111
    lamb biryani 115–16
    lamb haleem 54
    naan gosht 100–1
    paneer & cassava sizzler 87
    prawn jalfrezi 64
    red pepper chutney 137
    spinach, potatoes & peas 59
    sweet & sour prawns 77
    veggie biryani 102–3
    vegetable karahi 108
    vegetable noodles 89
    see also red onions
orange chili chicken 95

P

pakoras
    crispy pakoras 45
    salmon pakoras 46
paneer & cassava sizzler 87
peas
    creamy mixed vegetables 63
    keema pies 36–7
    spinach, potatoes & peas 59
    vegetable karahi 108
perfect curry spice mix 169
peri-peri sea bass 106
phirni rice dessert 157
piccalilli
    chicken & piccalilli squares 28–9
pies
    keema pies 36–7
pilau
    beef kheema pilau 104–5
pineapple
    pineapple chutney 136
    sweet & sour prawns 77
pink lamingtons 158–9

pistachios
    date & nut slices 15
    falooda 147
    rose & pistachio milk cake 162–3
pomegranate seeds
    lamb biryani 115–16
potatoes
    Bombay potatoes 62
    chana chaat 125
    chicken & piccalilli squares 28–9
    chicken & potato curry 117
    creamy mixed vegetables 63
    masala roast chicken & herby potatoes 72
    spicy potato & corn tortilla samosas 26
    spinach, potatoes & peas 59
    veggie biryani 102–3
    vegetable karahi 108
prawns see king prawns
puff pastry
    keema pies 36–7
    veggie pizza pinwheels 48

R

raspberries
    apple berry mocktail 141
red onions
    cauliflower Manchurian 93
    chana chaat 125
    chicken Balti 98
    classic kachumbar salad 122
    crispy pakoras 45
    prawn jalfrezi 64
    shakshuka 19
    spicy beef 82
    watermelon, feta & mint salad 124
    veggie pizza pinwheels 48
red peppers
    cauliflower Manchurian 93
    cheesy chicken muffins 20
    chicken Balti 98
    chicken bread rolls 50–1
    chicken chow mein 79
    Chinese-style spring rolls 47
    egg-fried rice 81
    jalapeño & chicken samosas 32–3
    keema pies 36–7
    lamb biryani 115–16
    paneer & cassava sizzler 87
    prawn jalfrezi 64
    red pepper chutney 137
    saucy gazebo chicken 84
    shakshuka 19
    spicy beef 82
    sweet & sour chicken 88

sweet & sour prawns 77
veggie biryani 102–3
vegetable karahi 108
vegetable noodles 89
veggie pizza pinwheels 48
rice
    basmati rice 132
    beef kheema pilau 104–5
    egg-fried rice 81
    khuri & khitchri 56–7
    lamb biryani 115–16
    lamb haleem 54
    veggie biryani 102–3
rice flour
    phirni rice dessert 157
    sweet & sour chicken 88
rose & pistachio milk cake 162–3
roti 126–7

S

saffron nan khatai 155
salads
    chana chaat 125
    classic kachumbar salad 122
    watermelon, feta & mint salad 124
salmon pakoras 46
samosas
    chicken & piccalilli squares 28–9
    how to fold 30–1
    jalapeño & chicken samosas 32–3
    spicy potato & corn tortilla samosas 26
saucy gazebo chicken 84
school dinner cake 156
sea bass
    peri-peri sea bass 106
semolina
    gulab jamun 161
    saffron nan khatai 155
sesame seeds
    Chinese-style spring rolls 47
    date & nut slices 15
    naan 130–1
    sweet & sour chicken 88
shakshuka 19
shortbread
    saffron nan khatai 155
sizzling lamb steaks 61
smoothies
    banana, date & oat smoothie 16
spice mixes
    bhuna masala 169
    meat biryani masala 169
    perfect curry spice mix 169
    vegetable biryani masala 169

spicy beef 82
spicy potato & corn tortilla samosas 26
spinach
    crispy pakoras 45
    spinach, potatoes & peas 59
spring rolls
    Chinese-style spring rolls 47
sticky lamb chops 80
stir-fries
    lamb stir-fry 90
strawberries
    nutty chocolate milkshake 144
    strawberry & watermelon refresher 140
sweet & sour chicken 88
sweet & sour prawns 77
sweet potatoes
    creamy mixed vegetables 63
sweet yogurt lassi 145

T

tomato passata
    beef kofta curry 112–13
    butter chicken 67
    king prawn & fish curry 111
    sticky lamb chops 80
tomatoes
    achari kheema 70
    beef bhuna 118
    butter chicken 67
    chana chaat 125
    chicken, cassava & corn casserole 69
    chicken & potato curry 117
    chicken Balti 98
    classic kachumbar salad 122
    folded omelet with cherry tomatoes & feta 17
    khuri & khitchri 56–7
    kidney bean curry 68
    king prawn & fish curry 111
    lamb haleem 54
    naan gosht 100–1
    paneer & cassava sizzler 87
    prawn jalfrezi 64
    shakshuka 19
    spinach, potatoes & peas 59
    tomato & cilantro chutney 133
    vegetable karahi 108
toor dhal (split pigeon peas)
    khuri & khitchri 56–7
tortillas
    spicy potato & corn tortilla samosas 26

V

vegetable biryani masala 169
vegetables
    creamy mixed vegetables 63
    veggie biryani 102–3
    vegetable karahi 108
    vegetable noodles 89
veggie pizza pinwheels 48

W

watermelon
    strawberry & watermelon refresher 140
    watermelon, feta & mint salad 124

Y

yogurt
    achari kheema 70
    beef bhuna 118
    chana chaat 125
    gulab jamun 161
    hariyali chicken 42
    khuri & khitchri 56–7
    lamb biryani 115–16
    mint & cilantro yogurt chutney 137
    naan 130–1
    sweet yogurt lassi 145
    veggie biryani 102–3

Z

za'atar
    fried eggs with peppers & za'atar 23

About the Author

Anisa Karolia is one of the United Kingdom's most popular Muslim food bloggers, sharing all of her favorite authentic recipes since 2015. She has a community of over 240,000 followers worldwide and was a British Muslim Award winner for digital activity in 2020.

Through her various platforms, Anisa's mission is to share quick-and-easy recipes, and she especially loves to share those all-time family favorites that she enjoyed growing up with.

www.cookwithanisa.com

🐦 @cookwithanisa
📷 @anisagrams
▶ @cookwithanisa

First published in Great Britain in 2023 by Ebury Press, an imprint of
Ebury Publishing.

For information about special discounts for bulk purchases, please contact
W. W. Norton Special Sales at specialsales@wwnorton.com or 800-233-4830

Manufacturing by Versa Press
Production manager: Devon Zahn

Book design by Studio Noel
Design: Studio Noel
Food stylist: Sonali Shah
Assistant food stylist: Kristine Jakobsson
Prop stylist: Morag Farquhar

Countryman Press
www.countrymanpress.com

An imprint of W. W. Norton & Company, Inc.
500 Fifth Avenue, New York, NY 10110
www.wwnorton.com

978-1-68268-894-6

10 9 8 7 6 5 4 3 2 1